For Martel, Greyson, and all children,
who deserve to be treated with respect and dignity

Parenting for Social Change

Parenting for
Social Change

Teresa Graham Brett

Published by Social Change Press, Learning Enterprises, LLC, Tucson, Arizona

Cover design by Jessica Castillo

Library of Congress Control Number: 2010919373

ISBN: 978-0-9829515-0-7

First U.S. edition 2011

http://www.parentingforsocialchange.com

ACKNOWLEDGMENTS

I have had so many teachers in my life who have challenged me to look beyond my unquestioned assumptions and find my true self. Martel and Greyson, the children who share my life, have taught me what it means to be a better parent and human being. I appreciate their willingness to be part of this book. Rob, my partner, was the first person from whom I experienced and continue to experience unconditional love and acceptance.

In my journey as a social justice educator, I owe a debt of gratitude to numerous individuals who helped to shape my understanding, challenge my biases and prejudices, and facilitate my growth as a human being. E. Royster Harper gave me the opportunity and support to be a part of the Intergroup Relations Program at the University of Michigan in Ann Arbor. Monita Thompson and Charles Behling were—and still are—companions in my learning journey. They pushed me to be my best self and see the world differently. I also deeply appreciate the many students with whom I worked at the University of Arizona, the University of Michigan, and the University of Texas at Austin, who shared their transformative learning processes with me and inspired my work.

As a writer and author, I want to thank those who supported me in my dream to write: Rob Brett, Donna Brett, Barb Lundgren, Sarah Parent, and Socorro Carrisoza. I am grateful to the support of fellow authors Lisa M. Cottrell-Bentley and Jan Hunt, who encouraged me to pursue publication of this book. I am grateful to the parents who read my website and share their stories of challenge and joy, and all the amazing parents I know who inspire me to continue my own journey by their commitment to treating children with respect and dignity.

Finally, I want to express my appreciation to Elizabeth Holaday, my editor. Her commitment to this project, persistence, direct feedback, and belief in the message of this book have helped to shape each of its pages.

CONTENTS

INTRODUCTION

I N THIS BOOK, I want to share with other parents my passion, knowledge, and skills for creating relationships with children from a foundation of respect and support rather than control.

The journey I've been on as a parent has been transformational in ways far beyond what I ever imagined. This ongoing journey has given me the opportunity to reflect deeply on my assumptions about parenting as I've strived to be a better parent. It's taken me on unexpected turns that have combined my professional experiences in universities with a deeper understanding of my role as a parent.

I invite you to join me on a similar journey. This journey requires us to go inward and examine the ways we learned about being a child when we ourselves were children. We'll look at how we may have been controlled as children. We'll examine our past and current social and cultural environments and consider how they shape our views as parents.

We'll look at why a belief that we must control children is harmful to their development as well as our own learning. We'll be challenged to look at patterns of behavior that are barriers to creating the respectful and supportive relationships we want with our children.

At times, this journey may seem like a leap of faith. We may have to face our fears about the future and the past. We may need to own all the parts of ourselves in our desire to honor all that our

1

children are. We do all of this to create for ourselves and our children a place where connection, love, respect, and understanding are the foundation upon which we experience the world.

The work we have to do is not about children. It's about us, the parents. Using self-reflection and a spiraling learning process, we can create a place where everyone's feelings, experiences, and voices are important, no matter what age. We can create a place where we can make a mistake and choose to learn from it because of our desire for connection, learning, growth, and understanding. We can create a place where everyone matters.

Through transforming ourselves and our family relationships, we can begin to create broader social change.

We'll be on this journey together, learning and unlearning, looking at our past to keep us in the present moment. By examining our past, we can acknowledge how our experiences as children—both good and bad—affect our current relationship with the children in our lives. In our desire to give children the same happy experiences we had or to avoid for them the painful experiences of our own childhood, we may miss the unique childhood that belongs to them.

I'll share with you some of the critical incidents and moments that helped me to see parenting beyond a control paradigm and to start moving toward respect and support. I'll bring to bear my professional expertise with creating environments for transformational learning. I'll share my successes and my failures, as well as my hopes and dreams. And I'll bring in other voices that can help us to reframe our thinking and challenge us to move forward.

Five years ago, I did not believe I was a controlling parent. It took a series of incidents, some of which I will share later, to open my eyes. Perhaps, like me, you don't think of yourself as controlling. You may believe, as I did, that control is necessary to ensure the safety and well-being of children. Just as I did, you may find yourself challenged to see your behavior as harmful—because, after all, you deeply love your children and only want the best for them.

I urge you to read on with an open mind and heart and to consider whether your good intentions may actually have harmful consequences for the child who shares your life.

We'll discuss in Chapter 1 how control operates in a larger context in our society. In Chapter 2, I'll describe some specific ways that children are often controlled. Some of this discussion may surprise you; I encourage you to suspend your previous notions of control and be willing to take a different look at how we might be controlling children even when we're not trying. Chapter 3 will look at the research into why control is harmful as well as what the research tells us about supportive parenting.

As we consider the ways that we control children, you may find yourself looking for solutions, for tools to avoid control and change your outlook. In Chapter 4, we'll move into the process of letting go of control and transforming ourselves to create different perspectives and relationships with children through our internal work as parents.

And finally, in Chapter 5, we'll discuss strategies for moving through our feelings as parents in order to create the opportunities children (and adults) need to learn and develop in ways that create a deeper connection to who they are as individuals and human beings.

The ideas and strategies in this book do more than create opportunities for children. They do the same for us, helping us to find the freedom to connect to who we really are. Ultimately, just as we are reflections of the world, the world is changed through our own transformation.

My Journey

In writing this book, I have included some anecdotes about my own experiences as a child, teen, adult, and parent. I grew up in a family of four. My family was bi-cultural, and as a child I was very much influenced by my mother's Japanese culture. My father was in the United States Air Force and met my mother while he was serving in Japan. They married, had my brother, and moved to the United States.

I was born in the U.S. and my family lived in various places in the U.S. and abroad during my childhood. We settled in Tucson when I was in 5th grade, and I met Rob, now my partner of 30 years, when I was in high school. After high school, I went on to university and then law school. Rob and I married when I was in law school and for several years we moved around the country, following my career.

Rob and I decided to have children when we were in our late 30's. Martel was born first and then Greyson almost five years later. As this book is being completed, they are nine and four years old.

While in law school, I decided not to practice law and instead went into higher education administration. I never took the bar or became licensed, much to my mother's dismay. I spent about 20 years working in universities and continue to work with universities and administrators as a consultant.

As an administrator and leader in universities, I made a professional commitment to try to make a difference in the experiences of college students who came from groups that had been marginalized in our educational systems and in our society at large. Through this work, I discovered a passion for challenging the ways we learn about the world that perpetuate stereotypes, biases, and discrimination based on different identities (such as economic class, sexual orientation, race, gender identity, age, national origin, ability status, language, or ethnicity).

One program that had a powerful effect on my outlook was a unique, transformative program with foundations in social justice education, psychology, sociology, and social psychology. It brought together students from different social identity groups to dialogue on challenging issues such as race, gender, and sexual orientation. Through these intergroup dialogues, students had the opportunity to examine their own beliefs and experiences as well as to learn from others in order to deepen their understanding of how to live and work across their differences and embrace their commonalities. I served as co-director of this program, which was developed at the University of Michigan, for six years.

In law school, I had visions of becoming the vice president of student affairs at a large public research university. I loved my work in universities, but as I came closer to this goal I found myself unhappy with the effects that working 60 hours a week had on my family and personal life. So although the opportunity to be exactly what I had dreamed of in law school presented itself while I was at the University of Texas at Austin, Rob and I decided to create a different life for our family.

We moved back to our hometown to be closer to our extended family and reinvent our lives. I started a higher education consulting business and found a passion for writing about social justice, social change, and parenting.

About this Book

The last thing the author of a book about social justice wants to do is use language that perpetuates cultural bias. As I wrote this book I became particularly aware of the fact that because I parent two boys many of the references and pronouns in my anecdotes are masculine. To balance this, I have used feminine pronouns throughout when referring to a hypothetical child or children in general.

I have also become sensitive to the words *my children*. Part of my process as a parent was the realization that I unconsciously felt that I had some ownership of my children and thus had the right to control them and determine how they should behave. As a result, I try not to use the words *my children*, but instead have shifted my thinking, talking, and writing to *the children who share my life*.

Also, while I recognize that all families are different, as all individuals are, I will often make references to *mainstream parenting*, by which I mean the typical parenting philosophies and practices of many American families across different cultural and socioeconomic groups. Mainstream parenting philosophy is influenced by the beliefs that childhood must be a long process of enculturation and socialization and that parents must use control to ensure that children successfully enter the adult world.

In mainstream parenting:

- children are viewed as adults-in-training;
- the focus is on the future, with the goal being to produce valuable adults;
- the child-parent relationship is secondary; and

- control is a necessary parenting tool that might include punishment (physical and/or verbal), shaming, and withdrawal of approval or expressions of love.

I was heavily influenced in the early days of my parenting by alternative ideas such as attachment parenting, exemplified by the parenting philosophy advocated by Dr. William Sears. Attachment parenting focuses on creating a bond between parents and babies or children through physical closeness (such as breastfeeding and co-sleeping) and responsiveness to crying and other cues.[1] Although I still believe in the importance of a strong bond and connection between parent and child, I have also come to question some of the ways control lurks beneath the surface of attachment parenting's tenets.

Because attachment parenting has also become accepted by so many in our society, it has become its own mainstream (though somewhat alternative) parenting culture. When any set of behaviors or beliefs becomes accepted without question, we may assume it is right without further examination. For this reason, alternative mainstream parenting may be just as problematic in its own way as traditional mainstream parenting, if we are not willing to critically examine its tenets.

What I advocate is a philosophy of parenting that is based on a child's right to respect and dignity, not a specific set of parenting behaviors that will guarantee a particular outcome. I advocate for operating from a frame of reference that holds that children deserve to be treated with the same level of respect as any other human being. In contrast to dominant mainstream parenting, I advocate parenting in which:

- children are viewed as full human beings, valuable in their own right;
- the focus is on the present, with the goal being to honor children's humanity;
- transforming the parent-child relationship can create broader social change, thus the child-parent relationship is primary; and
- the work we need to do is about ourselves as parents, not about changing children.

In order to achieve this frame of reference, it is critical that parents become aware of those behaviors and philosophies that are woven into the very cloth of our culture that deny respect and dignity to children. Questioning the necessity and value of these behaviors is the first step towards liberation.

This book is not like many of the parenting books that line bookstore shelves. I'm not going to tell you how to tame a toddler's tantrum or demand respect from a teenager. In some ways, this is a parenting book that isn't even about children—it's about the harmful cultural messages we, as parents, perpetuate in our relationships with children. And it's about the work we, as parents, must do to free ourselves, the children who share our lives, and our world from those messages.

CHAPTER ONE

Dynamics of Control

I N THIS CHAPTER, I want to place the issues of power and control over children within a larger societal context. Controlling children isn't just about the relationship between an adult and a child. It happens within a broader societal dynamic that is influenced by how we, as a culture, see children and the experience of childhood. Even though we may not see ourselves as controlling or mainstream parents, we can't help but be influenced by our culture in how we view our role as parents and how we use our power and our ability to control children.

When I use the terms *dominant mainstream parenting* or *paradigm of control and domination*, I'm referring to behaviors, beliefs, and attitudes that come from the assumption that adults are better than young people and, as a result, that we're entitled to act upon children and young people without their agreement. We believe in our right to grant and take away their privileges and to punish, threaten, hit, shame, and ostracize young people when we consider it beneficial in controlling or disciplining them.

Much of the control exerted on children is done in the name of caregiving. We control because we know that children's well-being is our responsibility and we have accepted without question that control is an integral part of fulfilling this responsibility. Let's begin to question that assumption.

Power versus Control

The words *power* and *control* are often used interchangeably, but in the language of sociology each has a distinct meaning. Power is the ability to take action,[1] whereas to control is to exercise direction over something or to dominate it.[2]

All human beings have some power to take action, but as adults we have more power than children. This power comes from our greater physical strength and the different ways in which we process information. We're also given power by the social structures in which we participate, such as schools and organized religion. Our legal system gives us power over children to determine what is best for them, within certain limitations, such as neglect and abuse. The legal doctrine of *in loco parentis* places schools in the position of parents with many of the same rights and responsibilities toward children.

The reality that adults have more power than children, however, does not mean that it is appropriate or necessary for us to exercise control over them. Rather, it means that we have an obligation to consciously choose how to use our power. We can choose to use our greater power to control children and coerce them to do what we want. We can choose to do nothing with our power. But we can also choose to use our power to support, assist, and facilitate the growth and learning of children in ways that affirm their personal power, dignity, and humanity.

Control as a Social Norm

The exercise of control over children is a process perpetuated by deeply-ingrained cultural beliefs about the nature of childhood. Throughout our lives, we are bombarded with information about how our culture views the world.[3] This information includes history, habits, and traditions, but it also includes biases, stereotypes, and prejudices,[4] usually connected to social identity groups. In the process of growing up we learn about ourselves not only as individuals, but also as members of social identity groups with particular roles in our broader society.

Although we may not think of children or youth as a social identity group, in reality childhood represents a unique identity group: the only group all people participate in, yet no one remains in. As a group, children are defined in contrast to adults; we make assumptions and reinforce stereotypes about youth and children that define their differences as deficiencies that must be overcome through a long socialization process carried out by parents, teachers, schools, and other individuals and institutions.[5] Further, the identities of children and childhood are constructed through the relationships developed between adults and children where adults control, for the most part, how the relationship is defined and how children are treated.

As babies we have limited information about the world, but we are born into cultures and societies with established cultural values, norms, and rules about appropriate behavior.[6] Individuals whom we love, trust, and depend on for our very survival shape our expectations, set out behavioral norms and rules, and pass on our culture's beliefs and standards.

The socialization (or enculturation) we receive growing up and as an adult happens at both an unconscious and a conscious level.[7]

It comes not only from other people, but also from the institutions we interact with, including schools, organized religion, television and media, businesses, and the legal and medical systems.

The dominant cultural view of children is that they are uncivilized, incompetent, and lacking in self-control. This attitude is reflected in the work of sociologists who, until the late 20th century, wrote of children needing to be moved away from nature (uncivilized, savage, exhibiting a lack of self-control) and toward culture (competent, reliable adults).[8]

This view of children is enmeshed with the dominant cultural view of parents. Just as we learn from our culture what it means to be a child, we are also guided by cultural beliefs as parents.[9] For example, we're socialized to believe that parents know what's best for children and that it's parents' responsibility to socialize children to fit the expectations and norms of our broader society.

Our culture—any culture—creates assumptions about the right way to parent.[10] The assumptions are implicit and, as such, are rarely questioned. Our socialization together with babies' dependency on us allows us to easily believe that we should control children's lives in order to ensure they turn out "right."

Because we are immersed in our cultural norms, we believe that we're doing the best thing for children when we make decisions for them. We accept from our own socialization that, for example, children are unable to decide the right foods to eat or the right times to eat. They can't be trusted to decide what to watch on television or what video games to play. They can't decide what time to go to sleep. We're convinced that because we've lived longer and have paid our dues, it's our right and our responsibility to make decisions for them.

Our control over children extends beyond issues of their health and well-being. As children grow, we reinforce their inferiority by trivializing their feelings. We'll say to teenagers that they have to wait until they're adults to do work that is important to them. When they take on serious issues we may diminish their efforts as juvenile and question their ability to make important decisions. We reinforce our lack of trust in them.

We generally don't see the control of young people as a problem, because we were controlled and dominated ourselves as children. It seems normal and expected because we have internalized and rationalized the use of control. We believe without question that it is necessary, and we believe it is the appropriate thing to do for children in our role as parents.

However, on reflection we can see that at the core of this paradigm is a lack of respect for children. They are treated as less important than and inferior to adults. We assume without evidence that they cannot be trusted to develop correctly, so they must be taught, disciplined, and punished in order to be guided into the adult world.

Creating freedom for children requires us to become aware and actively engaged in changing our beliefs and behavior. A good starting place is to consider and understand the dynamics of control in general and our particular experiences of control: how we were mistreated and devalued when we were children and how we act in ways that devalue the children in our lives.[11]

Questioning Control

In the United States, we often place value on the notion of freedom. But our history is full of examples of how the more powerful have denied groups of people the right to freedom and self-determination because of their so-called "deficiencies." At various points in our history, people of numerous ethnicities— African, Irish, Native American, Asian, Latino—as well as women; people with disabilities; individuals who identify as lesbian, gay, bisexual, or transgendered; and other social identity groups have been marginalized and discriminated against. Often, this discrimination was rationalized by beliefs that the marginalized groups were childlike, intellectually inferior, savage, or uncivilized.[12]

As a result of these beliefs, those in power often saw themselves in a paternalistic role.[13] This view begets a vicious cycle: if we view individuals and groups as inferior, we treat them as savage or uncivilized. They respond to this dehumanization by rebellion or through violence, and thus we rationalize the need to control their actions "for their own good." The cycle perpetuates the need to control and dominate those whom we deem inferior.[14]

Over the last two centuries we have come to some general understanding as a society that domination and control of groups of people based on ethnicity or gender is morally wrong. While discrimination undeniably persists, we have also generally accepted the falsehood of claims that these groups were savage or intellectually inferior. However, we have not yet extended this view to children and youth.

Even though I spent my professional life advocating for the empowerment of various social groups, I did not for many years recognize that I had internalized a dominant paradigm that disempowered children. Before beginning this transformational journey, I wouldn't have been able to admit that my control was harmful or diminished the children in my life in any way. The belief that children are inferior to adults was submerged in my subconscious. It was an implicit, unquestioned assumption. Because it seemed normal and natural to control, I rationalized my behavior and ignored Martel's protests.

I also implicitly believed that their dependence on me gave me the responsibility to mold Martel and Greyson. I experienced this training as a child myself. In my childhood, this molding was accomplished through control, fear, and violence, as well as threatened and actual withdrawal of approval and love. I was determined from the start not to use fear and violence with the children in my life, but I did not question the use of control, especially the kind of covert control favored by alternative mainstream parenting.

However, even if we don't use violence, control of children causes harm in the immediate parent-child relationship and disrupts the healthy emotional functioning of children. Control parenting, which is marked by feelings of less autonomy on the part of the child, is associated with antisocial behavior of adolescents and feelings of anxiety and anger in young adults.[15] We'll discuss the consequences of control parenting in much more detail in Chapter 3.

The ways children think and behave are not seen in the dominant culture as mere differences, but as defects that must be overcome through control. Ironically, it's this control of children that causes them to rebel, which, we believe, confirms our need to control them. We recreate the vicious cycle of control because of our belief that children are less than adults simply because they are different from us. If we did not see children as inferior to adults, we might not buy into the belief that children need to be controlled.

In my experience with Martel, the more I tried to control him, the angrier he became. His angry outbursts reinforced my belief that he needed me to control him because he could not control himself. When I let go of dominating him and treated him with the level of respect any human being deserves, his anger began to dissipate. My experience as a parent mirrored what I later read in research studies about the impact of controlling another person.

Instead of forcing my beliefs about who and what he should be onto him, I began to see myself as a partner and facilitator in his process. His voice, his ideas, and his concerns became more important to me and I began to step down from my role as dominator and oppressor. As a result, he began to respond with less anger to frustrating situations. We had started the process of disrupting the cycle of control. I began to see how I could use my power differently in my relationships with children.

Children *do* need our support and they *are* dependent. Their need to be cared for, however, doesn't give us the right to control their lives. Just as we have moved some distance from the belief that a wife should be controlled by her husband or that a woman who doesn't work for money has no right to decide how the money earned by her husband is spent, we can also begin to question the control of dependent children.

By examining the dynamics of control within the constructs of mainstream parenting, we can see larger patterns in our society that reinforce our perceived need to control children and our belief that this control serves to ensure their proper development. The relationship between an adult and a child is a reflection of the larger dynamics present in our mainstream culture. One of my goals is for us to uncover how our day-to-day interactions are defined by a paradigm of control and domination, and then to discover ways we can shed this paradigm for the sake of the children who share our lives.

CHAPTER TWO

Ways We Control Children

DURING THE LONG socialization process of childhood, those in authority (parents, teachers, clergy, schools, institutions, and others) pass down information and expectations about behavioral norms, values, and culture. Those who have more power impose their expectations about what is acceptable and appropriate, while those with less societal power may struggle against this control.

In this chapter I will give some examples of the ways we control children. Almost without exception, children's lives are more controlled than those of any other group in our society.[1] Adults impose limitations, judgments, and control on how children express their authentic emotions, on their bodies, on what food they eat and what media they interact with, on how they communicate with others, on how they learn, and on virtually every aspect of their experience.

Because control is considered a normal part of mainstream parenting, we may not think about the way we rationalize our control of children and believe it is helpful to their development. I know that earlier in my own journey I would have never considered some of my actions (both large and small) to be controlling. Even if I did acknowledge the methods of control I used, I believed the benefits of exercising control over Martel or Greyson outweighed any potential harm.

You may see yourself in some of these examples. That's a good thing; acknowledging the ways we use control is the first step towards creating non-coercive relationships. We'll talk in Chapter 5 about the feelings of guilt or anger that this recognition may provoke and about tools for turning away from control.

Alternatively, you may find yourself struggling to accept that some of the examples discussed here represent harmful uses of control, or you may feel that the exercise of control is sometimes unavoidable or the lesser of two evils. I will share some research throughout this chapter about why particular areas of control may not have the result we intend and may even be harmful, but for now, our goal is simply to recognize the control that we wield over our children, often thoughtlessly. We'll go on in Chapter 4 to discuss in more detail why that control may be harmful.

Emotional Expressions

In a culture that normalizes power-over and control of others, especially children, how a child communicates and expresses herself can become a battleground. One major responsibility given to parents of young children in mainstream parenting is to get children to control their emotional expressions, in particular perceived negative emotions such as sadness or anger. Mainstream parenting books and websites are filled with advice about how to tame temper tantrums and outbursts and how to prevent whining. We define some forms of expression as inappropriate, attempting to control the volume, words, tone, and duration of the ways children express emotions.

Some of the emotional controls encouraged by mainstream parenting are based on unquestioned cultural beliefs about child development. We may believe, for example, that older children should have outgrown the need to cry or should at least be able to control their crying. This belief leads many adults to feel immature or inadequate when they themselves cry. Similarly, in our culture boys are often discouraged from crying and are told from a very young age "big boys don't cry."

However, the primary cause of the adult desire to control children's emotions is probably that adults are not well-equipped to deal with our own emotions—having had our emotional expressions controlled as children. We recreate the controls imposed on us because we are uncomfortable with the feelings that arise when a child expresses her emotions.

As parents, we have no power to physically control a child's emotional expressions, even from birth. This is not true of many other behaviors; if a young child moves to hit someone, we can hold on to her fist or stand between her and her target. But if a child is crying, no matter how small she is, we have no physical control over that expression. This lack of power makes us deeply uncomfortable, since we have absorbed the cultural belief that we are supposed to be in control.

When a child is crying or angry in public, we are often even more uncomfortable because of our sense that we will be judged by others. When a child is sad, we may want to fix what is making her sad because we want her to be happy. If we're unable to make her feel better, we may feel uncomfortable with our inadequacy.

Our typical response to the discomfort provoked by children's emotional expressions is a desire to shut down the expression. We may do this directly ("stop crying!") or by trivializing the emotion, telling the child that she has no reason to be sad, despite the obvious reality of her sadness. Similarly, when an older child or teenager is moody, sullen, or withdrawn we judge those feelings and may isolate her or force her to behave in ways that are not true to how she feels. We may write off the feelings as being typical of teenage behavior, invalidating and trivializing the feelings and the individual.

Even when we accept the need for the expression of emotions, we may want to limit its length. At some point we think the child should feel better or that the expression is no longer authentic. I have often heard adults tell a child who has cried for a period of time, "Okay, you've cried enough; it's time to stop." This is another form of trivialization. The root of trivialization is anger: we are angry that the child is burdening us with her emotional expression "for no reason at all."

Notice that all of these reactions are based on the feelings that are triggered in the adult by the child's emotional expression. We feel sad, uncomfortable, or angry, and our response to those feelings is a desire to control the emotions of the child so that we ourselves can be more comfortable. In fact, we make the child responsible for our own emotions.

In my childhood, I often felt that I could express happiness or neutrality, but not anger or sadness. I've struggled ever since with feeling emotions such as sadness and anger because they were not acceptable in my childhood. Because of this experience, I decided early in my parenting that I wanted Martel and Greyson to have the freedom to express whatever emotions they were feeling.

In the early years of my parenting, when Martel was a toddler, I used covert control to create an environment in which there was little conflict between us. During this time, I found it easy to accept his range of emotional expressions. But as he got older, he and I experienced more and more conflict. He began to assert himself in ways that made me uncomfortable and angry.

As he got better at using words to articulate his needs and desires, I found them to be in conflict with my own desires for him. As his world grew larger and he began to interact with more children and extended family, I began to lose my covert control over what was coming in and out of the house.

I began to perceive a need to more actively control him. I could feel I was losing ground on my ability to control his environment so I began to set restrictions and conditions on behaviors such as how he spoke to me. Martel expressed a lot of anger at my overt controls.

Because of my own childhood experience, I wanted him to feel free to cry or express anger, sadness, or frustration without feeling that I disapproved. I didn't want him to censor his feelings in order to please me. Despite this, I often felt uncomfortable with how he expressed his emotions. I began to look for ways to control his emotional expressions through what I thought at the time was prevention. When he was angry at another child, for example, I would assume he was hungry or tired and would remove him or force him to eat.

I would help him process his feelings when I removed him from volatile situations. I wanted him to know he could talk to me about anything. What I did not do, at the time, was really look at the root cause of his anger. I would assume that it was about something— certainly not me!—that I could fix and control, and I would attempt to do that. I never considered that he felt controlled and manipulated by me, and what he really needed was to feel respected and in control of his own body, voice, developmental timeline, growth, and learning.

When Martel was almost five years old, I watched a video recording we had recently made. It showed a common scene, one I've seen in other adult/child interactions and obviously one that I've created myself. Martel was talking to me about something he wanted, using a tone of voice indicating that he was upset. Rather than listen to his concerns and feelings, I told him rudely and abruptly that I didn't like the way he was talking to me and that I expected him to talk to me in a different tone of voice, especially if he wanted me to respond to him. He became quiet. I had totally invalidated him and his feelings because he was using a tone of voice that I disliked.

My ideal vision of myself before Martel was born was of a loving, gentle parent who would accept him for who he was and kindly respond to any situation. The reality was that although I loved him deeply, just as my parents loved me, I set conditions on Martel in order for him to gain my approval and the outward expressions of my love, just as my parents had done. I used my power to control his emotional expressions.

As the adult, I have the power to set expectations that are most comfortable for me and best meet my definition of how a child should behave. I had recreated the same relationship with Martel that my parents had created with me and that I had observed in many other parent/child relationships.

I believe that my experience of being controlled emotionally as a child led to my discomfort with how Martel and Greyson express anger and sadness. I now see, though, that when I'm uncomfortable I can look at the reasons for my own emotions and choose not to recreate for them the same experiences I had as a child and continue to have as an adult. I can deal with my issues, rather than imposing my unhealthy reactions and patterns on them.

When we become uncomfortable with the way children express themselves, we may believe that we're sending a message that it's their behavior that we find unacceptable. Mainstream parenting philosophies claim to distinguish between the person (the child) and the behavior. Yet this distinction is too abstract for children, especially young children. Children equate their behavior, their feelings, and their experiences with themselves. Because of this, when we reject their behavior what children experience is a rejection of what they feel and, ultimately, who they are.

This is a difficult message to experience as a child. All children want the love and approval of their parents and will often do anything to ensure that they get them. When we, as parents, try to control a child's emotions, we strip her of who she is in that moment and require that she push her emotions down rather than allowing the feelings to flow.

We may believe that helping a child stop expressing emotions such as anger or sadness will help her develop greater self-control. She will then, we believe, be able to function more effectively as an adult. We may also choose not to see this as controlling or coercing her, instead believing that we are guiding her appropriately. With the best of intentions we may be trying to help children become healthy adults.

However, the unintentional message and impact of this control may be far more negative than we believe. When a child is allowed to express all emotions, including sadness and anger, and those emotions are allowed to run their course, the emotions dissipate and the child is better able to make sense of the experience. But by controlling how a child expresses her emotions, we require her to suppress them. When a child's perceived negative emotions are discouraged or suppressed by parents, researchers have found it has a negative impact on her competence outside the home, in both social situations and in task-oriented situations.[2]

This suppression of emotions does not allow the child to integrate the distressing experience and make sense of it. When she experiences a similar distressing situation, she relives the suppressed emotions of that past experience. We set up an emotional loop that becomes a pattern of behavior that is difficult to overcome. She is triggered by similar circumstances in the future—even as an adult—because the experience hasn't been integrated effectively.[3]

When we are uncomfortable with the ways a child expresses herself, rather than regarding the child or her behavior as the problem we have the opportunity to turn inward and see what it is within ourselves that makes us uncomfortable with others' expressions of emotions. In this way, we give ourselves the opportunity to grow and become more emotionally competent while we allow our children to grow and develop emotionally as well.

Bodies

Having control over one's own body seems a fundamental human right. In my work with university rape prevention programs, we told students over and over that "no means no," that each of us has the right to decide how and when our bodies are touched. I continue to feel passionate about the rights of women—indeed, all people —to say "no" and have their decision respected. Yet in our culture babies and children are not afforded the dignity of control over how they are physically treated.

We have conflicting cultural ideas about the sovereignty of children's bodies. We defend a child's right to freedom from unwanted and inappropriate sexual behavior, and we tell her that no one has the right to touch her inappropriately. However, we routinely disregard children's messages about how they wish to be treated. We force them to allow others to touch them in ways that we consider positive, we trivialize their physical discomforts, and, in some cases, we even inflict pain on them.

Like any aspect of enculturation, this disregard begins at birth. Before I had children, I was taught that babies are completely helpless and cannot communicate their needs until they are older. I learned through experience that in fact babies attempt to the best of their physical ability to control or avoid uncomfortable situations. A baby will avert her eyes, turn her head, squirm, or cry when faced with an objectionable interaction.

Often parents of a baby who doesn't want to be held by strangers are encouraged to let others hold her anyway, so that she will be "less shy." She's not accepted for who she is and what her preferences are if these preferences go against what adults want from her.

As she gets older, we have expectations about how she will physically interact with others. The underlying assumption is that, as adults, we have the right to control a child's body because she is smaller and doesn't know how to behave appropriately. Adults, who have more power, may require her to hug a relative or friend, to shake hands with a stranger, or to allow people to pinch her cheeks, pat her head, or touch her in other ways. For a child, a hug or even a handshake can feel overwhelming, invasive, and inappropriate (in fact, some adults have the same experience). Too often, however, a child's reluctance to engage others physically is seen as a deficiency that must be overcome by force.

If we reinforce the idea that a child's perspective, voice, and comfort are less important than an adult's, then we send the message that her body is not hers to control. She must endure her personal discomfort because adults, who are larger and more powerful than her, require her to do so.

Medical and dental exams are often presented to children as something they must cooperate with for their own good, regardless of their feelings about the experience. Before Martel's first "solo" visit to the dentist, when office rules required that I not stay with him during the exam, I spoke privately with the office manager, insisting that Martel had to be the person in control of his own body. I pointed out to her that many adults, including dentists and doctors, do not respect a child's decision when they ask for a procedure to be stopped. She replied, "Of course, we would stop," but I felt I was being patronized.

I said, "When he says 'no' that has to be respected."

She stepped back with a look of recognition and said, "Oh… it's like if a woman says 'no', it means 'no'."

"Yes," I responded, "it's exactly like that."

"I get it now," she said. "I have goose bumps from even thinking about it that way."

From her comment, I knew that she understood that Martel had the absolute right to stop any procedure that made him uncomfortable. She was able to connect to her prior understanding of a woman's right to be in control of her body and I felt as though she had reached a genuine understanding rather than simply saying the words to placate an "overprotective" mother.

In addition to coercing children into accepting physical contact with others, it is normal in our culture to trivialize their physical discomforts. Charles Darwin, echoing an understanding typical of his time, grouped "animals, children, savages, and the insane" together in determining that they did not have an awareness of pain.[4] This may sound like a bizarre notion to us today, but the idea that children's experiences of pain are somehow less than adults' persists.

It was not until 1987 that the American Academy of Pediatrics endorsed the use of anesthesia for newborn surgical procedures.[5] In a 1996 survey of over 3000 U.S. physicians, the Academy found that only 45% of doctors performing circumcisions used anesthesia or analgesia.[6] Even with anesthesia, circumcision results in significant pain, but the myth that babies don't feel pain or at least do not feel it in the way adults do persists, allowing many parents to choose to circumcise boys without regard to the pain it inflicts.[7]

Even adults who believe that children do feel pain often minimize their experience. It is commonplace to hear a parent tell a child to "get over it" or that it is "not so bad." Most people would never tell an adult friend "it doesn't hurt," yet children are routinely told that their pain is not real.

We also use terms that minimize children's physical domination. Corporal punishment is not called *hitting*, it's called *spanking*. We "swat" a toddler on the butt. Even when a child is raped, we most often refer to it as *sexual abuse* or *molestation*. Although these are legal definitions, it is revealing of our culture that we don't use the same powerful words when children are violated that we use when adults are.

The issue of control and power over a child's body clearly extends to physical punishment. Within our paradigm of control and domination, although the right of adults to hit children has come under more scrutiny, hitting or spanking a child is still often considered acceptable. Yet no experience could more clearly express to a child that her body is not her own to control than having a loved and trusted parent deliberately inflict pain on her.

Like many or even most adults of my age, I was physically punished as a child. Time out was not the punishment of choice at that time. My father whipped me with a belt. I still remember getting whipped and frankly it did not, in any way, ensure that I would behave better. What I got better at was hiding those things that I knew my parents would be upset about. It created resentment and anger on my part. It did not make me respect my father more, although I did fear him when he'd been drinking or was angry.

The humiliation I experienced as a result of those whippings would stay with me. I hated the feeling that someone could decide what to do with my body and I had no control over it because that person was bigger and stronger than me.

One night, Rob and I were changing clothes. I was sitting on the bed and Rob was standing nearby. He pulled his belt off quickly with one hand, and I instinctively ducked, filled briefly with an overwhelming fear. That motion was exactly what my father would do when he was angry and getting ready to whip me or my brother. I was in my early 30's, yet that motion—even by my loving partner—was enough to take me back to my childhood fear.

Despite seeing my childhood experiences as negative, I've still struggled with not using my physical size to impose my will on Martel and Greyson. It can be easier with a toddler or small child who doesn't comply with a request to physically overwhelm her in order to get compliance.

The world is naturally full of limitations for a child. At a young age, a child needs to feel like she is big and can control as much of the world around her as possible. All children strive to have mastery and control of the world around them. To some degree, all children are frustrated, humiliated, and threatened by finding out that they don't have that mastery.[8] Some frustrations come from natural limitations in the world, others are imposed by adults.

It's my responsibility to find ways for the children who share my life to successfully navigate the physical world. Unfortunately, during times of stress, I can forget this and become frustrated and impatient. I then fall back into my socialization and impose myself on Martel or Greyson in order to accomplish whatever it is I'm trying to get done, whether it is getting someone dressed more quickly, putting on shoes, or changing a diaper.

Some might think that forcing a toddler to change her diaper by physically restraining her does not fall into the same category as hitting her. Both, however, involve enforcing compliance through physical means, and both are permitted by our belief that we have the right to control the body of a child. Of course, hitting a child is never necessary, while it can be important to change a soiled diaper at some point for a child's health. Yet rarely—or never—is the urgency to change a diaper genuinely brought on by health concerns. Most often, the urgency comes from the parent's desire to take care of the chore at a convenient time and place.

In addition to the underlying cultural belief that parents and other adults have the right to control a child's body, mainstream parenting philosophy holds that it is our responsibility to exercise our power so that a child learns what's right and wrong. This responsibility may mean the use of physical force and is frequently a justification of physical punishment. But do children really learn right and wrong from coercion and punishment?

Research tells us they do not. By using an adult's physical size to force a child to do something she doesn't want to do or to punish her, we're actually teaching her that if you're stronger than someone else you can force her to do what you want rather than working together to find common ground.

A child who is harshly punished learns that physical violence can be used to change others' behavior. She is less likely to learn nonviolent conflict management skills.[9] Ironically, we most often use physical punishment in response to a child's aggression—modeling the very behavior we're trying to eliminate. In a number of studies, experiencing physical punishment was "significantly related to adult involvement in intimate violence."[10] Physical punishment as a child has also been associated with depression in adulthood.[11]

Even though as parents we may feel it's our obligation to teach our children to regulate their actions and anger, our control has unintended consequences. None of us hopes to create dysfunctional, depressed adults! Yet despite what we are told by mainstream parenting books and websites, controlling parenting methods aren't about raising children to be healthy, functioning adults. They are really about soothing our own discomfort and meeting the expectations of a broader social structure.

Food

We've all seen information in the news and from doctors and other health professionals about the rising rates of obesity in children and the increases in childhood diabetes. Many children and adults in our society struggle with food and body image issues.

As parents, we may be prey to enormous anxiety around what our children eat. When a child refuses to eat certain foods, or eats less than we think she should, we worry. If she eats too much or chooses foods we call "junk," we worry. We may work very hard as parents to provide nutritious meals only to have a child reject them. We may see food not eaten as a waste of money or of natural resources.

We all absorb cultural messages about food and eating, just as we do about all aspects of our culture. Our parents may have used food as a punishment, reward, or bribe. Food may have symbolized love or comfort. We may see some foods as virtuous and some as a guilty pleasure. Our parents may have forced us to sit at the table and finish our dinner before we could have dessert. If we refused to eat our meal, perhaps it was saved to be eaten later before any other food. The messages we absorb become part of our belief system and, if left unquestioned, may be passed on to our children as well.

How to handle food and eating with Martel and Greyson was (and sometimes continues to be) a struggle for me as a parent. I had the best intentions, wanting them to be healthy and knowing that diet affects wellness in many ways. During my first pregnancy I read about all the things I could do to make sure Martel would eat and want healthy foods. No sugar for the first three years, according to Dr. Sears[12], would ensure he wouldn't crave sweet foods. I devoured this advice and other tips like it.

When Martel was a baby, I trusted him to nurse on demand, but at the time I would never have dreamed of trusting his ability to choose when and what he wanted to eat as he grew older.

I asserted my need to control through the food my family ate: no fast food, no "junk" food, only one piece of a sweet or sugary treat and only once in a while. When I look back at this need to control, I know that so much of it was a desire to regain the power I lost as a child. I still struggle with this loss and have to work to not use the loss of control over my own life as an excuse to exercise it over those around me.

As Martel grew older and began to assert his autonomy and independence, I projected many things onto him. When he bristled at my control, I was sure that his anger and outbursts were the result of low blood sugar or eating the wrong thing. It would not occur to me until almost a year later that his anger could be the result of being oppressed by me.

I was such a dominating force in Martel's life during this period that one time when his aunt offered him goldfish crackers and asked how many he wanted, he lacked any ability to make the decision for himself. He became so overwhelmed and frustrated that he sat in the kitchen corner and cried because I was not there to tell him how many he could have. He was four at the time. I had completely stripped him of his inner authority when it came to making decisions about food, and he could barely function without me there.

I controlled Martel's food with the best of intentions. I would never have believed that I was setting him up to have an unhealthy relationship with food, because I had his best interests at heart. And yet, my control of his food could have had far-reaching consequences that I had not anticipated.

In looking at the impact of parental influence on children's eating behaviors, researchers have found that restricting access to certain foods and pressuring a child to eat more might have the short-term result of getting a child to comply with the parents' expectations. However, in the long term coercion and control have the opposite effect. For example, when access to food is restricted, there is evidence that in the long term children tend to eat when not hungry, do not have the ability to self-regulate their diet, and tend to gain weight as well as have a negative self-image.[13]

During those times when I was controlling food in our family, I wouldn't have characterized my behavior as coercive. Once I began to shift my view of children, I saw my behavior for what it truly was.

About a year after Martel gained some freedom from my control, he asked me to make him a pop tart and egg toast. I made the pop tart, then the toast. I sat down to eat my own breakfast at the table and he was watching television and eating while standing up. At first I was casually watching him; then I really observed what he was doing. I saw the joy with which he ate both the pop tart and the toast. He would pick up the piece of pop tart or toast, look at it, decide where to bite and chew slowly. He then would look again at exactly where he wanted to bite, take the bite, and chew.

He was so joyful. He was in a state of grace, eating exactly what he wanted, the way he wanted. Today, he eats only what he wants. He listens to his body when he is full. He is not full of shame and guilt. He has wisdom that I can only hope to regain. I am sure I had it once, but I was not trusted to know myself and my body. And I have continued to live the legacy of distrust.

As more time has passed, Martel has become so amazingly clear about what he wants. He won't eat any food just to eat something. If it doesn't taste right to him, isn't exactly what he wants, he doesn't finish it. Traditional control parenting, the kind that perpetuates power-over dynamics, would tell me I am creating a picky eater. What I see is that he eats exactly the right food at the right time for his body.

Even as I have reveled in his connection to the needs of his body, I have also struggled to continue to go beyond what I learned about the role of adults in determining what and how children eat. Several years after I let go of controlling food, an incident came up where Martel had been asking for lots of different kinds of food, only to eat one or two bites and then tell me that he must have been wrong about wanting it. I started feeling a lot of frustration and eventually made a comment to the effect of, "Well, that's what usually happens with you. You don't want whatever you've asked for."

This comment wasn't made in an observational way, but in a judgmental way. I was clearly expressing my disapproval of his actions. Martel's reaction—apologizing somewhat desperately—made it clear that I had hurt him and that he felt he had to regain my love and approval.

As I took in the impact of my words, I knew that what was more important than my inconvenience was that Martel maintain his healthy relationship with food. I truly didn't want him to force himself to eat something that he did not like, just so I wouldn't feel inconvenienced. This result would have been exactly the opposite of what I wanted for him!

The cycle of control has lifelong consequences. Even as adults, we still live with the effects of the control adults exercised over us as children. A critical and coercive family environment is one dynamic that is considered instrumental in the development of an eating disorder.[14] People with eating disorders often describe their struggles with food as going back to their childhood dinner table and the control their parents tried to exercise over what and how they ate from a young age.[15]

We lose our power as children. In its place we are taught by people who love us and who are in positions of authority that we should do what they say in order to successfully gain their love, approval, and trust. Our own inner authority, our knowledge of ourselves and our bodies, is replaced by outer authority figures.

If we focus on fear for our children's future, such as fear that they may develop eating habits that will impair their future health, we may feel that the issue of what to eat is too important to allow our children to be in control. However, it is precisely because food and eating are of such lifelong importance that we must be cautious not to damage our children's ability to attend to their inner authority. Our bodies are remarkably able to guide us in choosing a healthy balance—if we don't learn to ignore their signals in favor of external authorities and rote rules.

In addition to struggling with my role in Martel and Greyson's eating, I've also struggled with the impact on my own eating of disengaging from my body and not listening to its signals. I sometimes eat beyond when I'm full. I sometimes eat things I don't really want. I'm trying to regain clarity about what and when my body needs to eat, with Martel and Greyson as my models.

As parents we receive the message that children don't have the ability to self-regulate and it's our responsibility to do this for them. If we're to ensure that they grow up eating healthy foods, we must restrict, control, and/or coerce. But these methods have exactly the opposite effect.

A child whose eating is controlled in some way by her parents loses her ability to self-regulate, and her desire for the "forbidden food" increases. We then observe her inability to self-regulate and decide that we must control her further, and the vicious cycle of control goes on. We must challenge our commonly-held assumptions about control and self-regulation in order to give children the freedom to develop their own ability to self-regulate.

Media

In our desire to create a healthy environment for children, we may have read and thought about the dangers of violent, frightening, or sexually-suggestive television, video games, and other media. Aside from concerns about content, we may feel that such media are at best empty entertainment, in contrast to activities we believe to be educational or enriching. When I began to deeply examine the ways I used my power to control and dominate Martel's life, I realized that much of my desire to control came out of fear. This was true of food control and it was also true of the control I imposed on Martel's media access.

I'm not talking about the kind of instinctual fear we feel when we see a child running for a busy street, but rather fear about some imagined future. I believed and feared that if Martel watched violent shows or played violent video games he would internalize the violence and become violent himself. I had accepted and internalized the belief that children could not distinguish between real life and TV.

When Martel was a toddler, I would observe other children who watched shows I deemed violent and look for confirmation in their play that they were indeed becoming violent themselves. I had accepted the idea that children needed regulation because they couldn't make the right choices for themselves. I definitely had lots of biases about what types of shows and videos Martel should watch. I truly believed that controlling his access to certain kinds of media was for his own good, to protect him from bad influences or from being frightened.

Living from this place of fear moves us out of the present relationship we're creating with the children in our lives and propels us into a future where we imagine the worst possible outcomes. Too often, our socialization—which has fear at its center[16]—doesn't allow us to observe a situation from a neutral perspective and so we miss critical information.

I remember when I first decided to introduce the Star Wars trilogy to Martel when he was four or five years old. I had them on VHS and over the course of my life had watched them countless times. I decided that while Martel could watch most of the original trilogy, I wouldn't let him watch two scenes that were particularly scary and disturbing. Rather than telling him that I felt the scenes were too frightening for him, however, I also decided to tell him that I myself was disturbed by the scenes and didn't want to see them.

One day Martel was in the bedroom watching the movies while recovering from a cold. I heard one of the forbidden scenes coming up and told Martel I was coming in to fast-forward the VCR. As I went toward the room, Martel slammed the door, held it closed and yelled, "Mom, don't worry, the scene's almost over, and then you can come in." As it turned out, he wasn't scared at all by what was happening in the movie. Had I discussed the scenes with him honestly, I might have realized that they would not frighten or upset him. But my fear for him did not allow me to even consider that he could handle them.

When I began to awaken to my control and domination, I read numerous articles from parents who didn't control their children. They introduced me to the idea that I could trust Martel and, later, Greyson to know when they had reached the edge of their comfort level.

With this in mind, I began to observe, in a neutral way, Martel's reactions to television shows or movies, and I realized that sometimes he did indeed get scared and want to change the channel or leave. But what scared him was not what I would have assumed. The common theme was a child who was getting into trouble and would soon be scolded or punished by adults. He also didn't like shows where children or teenagers were in danger.

If he saw something that made him uncomfortable, he would ask me to change the channel or turn off the show. Thinking about this, I realized that all along he'd been communicating his comfort level to me, and that even while I had complied with his requests I hadn't made the connection that he was in fact self-regulating his access to media.

Because my socialized worldview was that I couldn't trust Martel to judge his own comfort level, I missed the truth about his abilities. It was right in front of my eyes, but I didn't trust Martel or what I saw. And because I was socialized to believe that I knew what was best for him, I made wrong assumptions about what he would find frightening or disturbing.

As I let go of controlling Martel's media access, I began watching television with him much more often. At first I disliked many of the shows. I disdained them because they were filled with fighting and battles. Ironically, I love watching period movies with lots of fighting and battles, but I wouldn't question my love of these movies because I'm an adult and of course I trust my own ability to distinguish between reality and fantasy.

At first, I was unable to extend this trust to Martel, and so I saw the fighting in shows he liked differently. But when I began to look more deeply at the themes depicted in the shows, I saw that they were portraying strong young people who made a difference in their worlds.

These characters often have special powers they use to save the world or battle evil. Adults in these shows often depend on the younger characters to save their communities. The kids in these shows are not relegated to just going to school and doing what adults tell them to do. They are powerful, smart, and self-actualized. They do important things. I gained a great appreciation for The Kids Next Door, who actually declare their mission is to battle adult tyranny! When I controlled what Martel watched, I didn't feel the need to watch television with him. However, our relationship has been enriched through watching these shows together. I feel that I have gained insight into what is going on for him when we talk about the shows and share the experience. His world opens up to me in ways it hadn't when I was unwilling to give up control over his choices.

Occasionally, there are instances in which some shows reinforce paradigms and stereotypes around gender, race, body size, or sexual orientation that are difficult for me. Part of my challenge when this happens is to remain in mutual dialogue with Martel, as opposed to lecturing him about my views of right and wrong. I feel strongly about eliminating oppression on the basis of sexual orientation, race, gender, and other social identities. Still, inquiring about how Martel might be experiencing a character or show, rather than just telling him what I think, can open up a dialogue that creates trust and respect as it engages both of us in a critical analysis of our experiences.

If, instead, I choose to impose the "right" values on "my" child, I merely reinforce through my actions that the individual or group in power has the right to define the truth. To impose my truth on Martel and force him to believe—or act like he believes—what I do would be a violence perpetrated on him, all in the name of justice.

Concern for media violence typically includes video games as well as television. Some well-publicized studies have appeared to demonstrate a correlation between violent video games and violent acts in children, leading many parents to regard video games with fear. However, much of the research on the possible connection between game violence and actual violence has not taken into account family violence or aggressive personalities. When these factors are taken into account, studies show that violent video games and other media may actually have only a limited role or no role in causing violence.[17]

Other research has shown that violent video games may actually play an important, positive role in the development of adolescent boys.[18] Just as physical play allows children—often boys—to explore aggression and dominance without actual harm, video games allow them to safely explore issues of death, war, and violence. Boys in a cross-racial study were found to use violent video games to explore and master exciting and realistic environments, explore fantasies of power and glory, and to work out feelings of stress and anger. The boys in the study could also clearly distinguish between fantasy and reality.[19]

Beyond concerns about violence, there is a mainstream view of entertainment-based video games as antithetical to learning. When children and teens play video games, parents often view it as a waste of time and a barrier to learning. However, research calls this assumption into question as well.

One study looked at what it means to gain expert knowledge in any subject matter. It identified common characteristics of experts in various fields, among them superior short-term and long-term memory, the ability to solve problems quickly, seeing and representing problems at a deeper level than novices, and excellent self-monitoring skills.[20]

Comparing children who were outstanding video game players to adult experts in other fields, the researchers found that

The evidence indicated that they demonstrate many expert behaviors. [Highly skilled child players] in this study demonstrated the following behaviors at advanced levels within the scope of the game environment: actively seeks new information; incorporates new information; assesses situations using multiple pieces of data; organizes, classifies, and categorizes information; consistently applies successful behaviors; is confident about one's own knowledge; is willing to take risks; employs corrective action when needed; can consider input from multiple sources; recognizes patterns; uses holistic thinking; is able to integrate information with behaviors; uses inductive thinking; strategizes; thinks critically; and recognizes constraints and misinformation.[21]

This study clearly indicates a greater role for video games than simply being a way to pass the time or to develop eye-hand coordination.

We may choose to see video games as a waste of time for children. We may decide to limit the number of hours children play or the types of games they play because we believe they must engage in activities that are more productive. If we are able to shift our view and consider video games from a more neutral perspective, we might see a positive role for video games and other media in the lives of children. By pre-determining our views, we miss an opportunity to understand how video games impact children beyond fears of violence and lack of educational value.

Moving away from our commonly-held beliefs about our need to control children in order to ensure they learn how to function properly in the world creates an opportunity to see the experiences they engage in through a different lens. If we are sure we know what the outcome will be from a particular activity, like watching television or playing video games, we miss the chance to see what is really happening in the lives of the children with whom we live.

Knowing Our Children

The privilege and power I have as an adult often obscure the ways in which I use domination and control. When we are within the control paradigm, our ability to see our behavior objectively is diminished. Stepping outside the paradigm to view our behavior with a different perspective is difficult,[22] but essential to treating children with dignity.

In our interactions with children, there are times when we are explicitly trying to fulfill our systemic responsibility to mold their behavior so that they're socially acceptable. In an effort to civilize and tame children, we often try to control them through the belief that we know them better than they know themselves.

Other times the same belief causes us to unintentionally disregard and diminish children. When we intrude on their private thoughts and feelings, for example, we strip them of their right to be separate individuals and to be in control of how they share information.

This disempowerment, whether intentional or not, is often seen as a normal part of childhood. When teenagers begin to rebel and reject their parents' control and domination, this is seen as a normal rite of passage. This rite of passage may be seen as "normal" because we haven't challenged the notion that children cannot be trusted and adults must control them.

Martel once let me know that he needed to call a friend to tell him about his newest trading cards. I said, "is there something else you wanted to talk to your friend about, maybe getting together to play?". He smiled and nodded. I said, "I knew you wanted a playdate! I could just tell." Martel's smile turned into a frown and he began to cry. He told me that when I say those kinds of things he feels that he can never have any thoughts to himself; he could have no secrets. He left the room upset and sad.

Of course, I apologized. I felt bad that I'd hurt him. Then I went into victim mode for a few minutes, feeling sorry for myself that Martel was so "sensitive" to the things I said. I could just never please him, I thought. I was transported back to my childhood where I felt as though whatever I did wasn't good enough to maintain the love and acceptance of my parents.

Later that day, I began to reflect on our conversation. I realized that my socialization as a child had taught me that parents or adults supposedly know children better than they know themselves. We learn at a young age to substitute the knowledge and authority of others (in particular parents, teachers, and other adults) for our own knowledge and authority.

As adults and parents, this socialization continues and we are further indoctrinated to believe that responsible parents use their superior knowledge and wisdom to teach children, not only about themselves, but also about how they need to act in order to be productive and fit the norms of our society.

In light of my socialization and experiences, I believed at the time that my comment to Martel was made in a loving and fun manner. Between individuals who have a more equal power relationship, the kind of statement I made might have been experienced as I had intended. But Martel's honest reaction to what

I said clearly demonstrated that my intent didn't match the impact of my statement. The reality is that what I said was disempowering and belittling. What I'd done in that statement was to use my power over Martel to show him that he couldn't think of anything that I had not already thought of.

At the time, he wasn't ready to share with me that he wanted to play with his friend. I had pre-empted him and robbed him of his ability to inform me of what he wanted in his own time and his own way. Although each of us wants to be known and loved for who we really are, we also have the right to decide the ways in which we choose to reveal ourselves to those around us. Just because I think I know what Martel is thinking, feeling, or planning, I don't have the right to use my power as a parent to demonstrate this "knowledge" in ways that disempower him.

There are times when I try to give voice to an emotion Martel might be feeling. When I've done this in an empowering way, his reaction is very different, often a sense of relief that I might understand what he is going through. He may continue the conversation and ask me if I felt the same way as a child. These conversations deepen our relationship of trust because I work to minimize the power imbalance between us. I make myself Martel's partner and explore the similarities and differences of our experiences, rather than using my authority as an adult to define his experiences for him.

Although I work to compensate in our relationship for the power differential between child and adult, I must remain vigilant about the ways I unintentionally disempower the children who share my life. This conversation was another opportunity to reflect on how I have accepted the dominant paradigm of control and power over children and perpetuated the system of oppression unknowingly, at least in the moment.

Social Skills

Our role as parents in a society that views children as adults-in-training includes the responsibility to teach children proper social skills. The majority of parents, regardless of their parenting style, have some hope that their children will care about others, be empathetic, be a good friend and partner, and be happy. I have not met one parent who hopes to raise a child to become a self-centered, angry, and anxiety-ridden adult. Our dominant view of childhood emphasizes the forced learning of social skills such as sharing, politeness, and negotiation and compromise.

Like any parent, I want Martel and Greyson to be able to navigate social situations and be comfortable in a wide variety of settings. I hope that they will be able to establish social relationships with other children and adults, as they desire. What I've come to question, in looking at the ways we control and coerce children, is whether mainstream parenting methodologies are appropriate or even effective at achieving this goal.

Common mainstream advice to parents is to ignore or correct a child who doesn't use the socially-accepted words or tone of voice. If a child doesn't use the "magic words," we're told we should correct her or we'll reinforce her unacceptable behavior. If we respond to a child when she's whining, we're told that she'll learn to whine to get what she wants. How might children experience this correction? Is it likely to make them feel genuine appreciation?

When out one day with Greyson, I went to a grocery store that gave out balloons to children. He asked if I would get him a blue one. We approached the staff person blowing up balloons and I asked, "Could we have a blue balloon?". The person replied, "What is the magic word?".

I was taken aback. Of course, I've heard this phrase, or others like it, directed at children on countless occasions. As the adult to whom this was directed, I felt angry, humiliated, and incredibly frustrated. A rush of emotions washed over me and I felt as though I had been transported back to childhood—in spite of the fact that the conversation was between two adults.

I have no memory of being told this as a child, although perhaps I was. The experience, however, gave me some small insight into how a child might feel because of the enormous power differential between adults and children. A simple request becomes fraught with humiliation.

In our dominant mainstream culture, we rarely question being rude to children. This is ironic, since we insist on polite behavior from children and in fact are often rude to them with the goal of teaching them to be polite. We'll tell a child in front of other people that she must say "please" or "thank you." Imagine for a moment correcting your partner or an adult friend if she or he neglected to say "please" in a store. Few of us would do so, yet we'll interrupt and correct a child who doesn't "properly" make a request of an adult.

I've also heard older children enforcing these expectations on younger children. Children can very quickly internalize the domination they experience and in turn impose it on others who are younger and less powerful than they are.

We may also be rude to children out of simple disregard for their feelings or privacy. For example, we'll often share personal information about a child with others without asking her permission. There are times when I want to share a story about Greyson or Martel with a friend, but I learned early on that while these stories may be cute to me, they are potentially embarrassing to them. Now, if I want to share something I ask first if it is acceptable, as I did for the anecdotes in this book.

We may fear that if we don't force children to be polite, they'll never learn how to treat others with kindness, politeness, and compassion. However, coerced "magic words" are rarely sincere. The words *please* and *thank you* can be used to express genuine politeness and caring, but they can also be a mask for resentment and sarcasm. Similarly, when I've heard children being forced to apologize, I've rarely, if ever, heard a genuine apology. What children learn from the experience of coercion is that adults, who have more power, can rudely (and disrespectfully) force them to do things that are disingenuous. This hypocrisy is not lost on children.

If we look beyond the need to use specific words, we can see that children are often genuinely polite and appreciative. A child who shows excitement at receiving a gift by jumping up and down or flashing a huge smile is expressing authentic gratitude, yet too often she learns that her expressions of appreciation don't meet the standards of adults. She is told to say "thank you" even when her demeanor, her eyes, and her excitement have already genuinely expressed her appreciation.

In our home, we don't require anyone to say the words *please* or *thank you*. However, we often do use those words. Sometimes we're more blunt in stating our needs, other times more polite. We try to create room for wherever people may be at a given moment and do our best to give each other the benefit of the doubt.

Another imposition on children in mainstream parenting that is not applied to adults is the requirement to share belongings. We believe that if children don't learn to share, they'll become selfish and self-centered adults. However, when we recognize that adults who prefer not to let others use their things are not held to this same standard, we can begin to question the appropriateness of forcing children to share.

Greyson received a birthday gift one year and wanted to play with it right away. There were other kids there, and he was willing to share his other toys but not this new toy that seemed to feel very special to him. I overheard a comment from another adult to the effect that Greyson should share his new toy. Yet this same adult, I also overheard, wasn't willing to let an older child use her new computer. Somehow we expect children to share their things, no matter how new or special, but we don't expect adults to do the same.

The fact that we accept behaviors in adults that we don't consider socially acceptable in children is emblematic of our belief that children don't need to be treated with respect. This disempowerment is justified by our perceived need to teach children good manners. However, in the wide range of research on control of children I have yet to find any that shows positive outcomes from this control. The impacts are almost always the opposite of what parents intend.[23]

Research looking at perceptions of control showed that young adults who had been controlled by their mothers were less empathetic as adults.[24] We want our children to be empathetic and caring, often seen as the hallmarks of a good friend. We feel compelled to ensure they grow up to be polite and caring by controlling how they express these traits as children—yet we may be creating the very outcome we were trying to avoid.

Manipulation

Mainstream parenting books and websites often dedicate a great deal of space to the ways children try to manipulate adults and push boundaries. Our culture labels children—even babies—as manipulative. The issue of manipulation is usually couched as one-way: children manipulating adults. When those who have more societal or institutional power manipulate others, it's unremarkable; when those who have less societal power manipulate others, it is a threat to the paradigm of control and must be curbed.

Other disempowered groups are also often accused of manipulating those in power. For example, as a university administrator, I heard more times than I care to remember that a student of color was using the "race card" to manipulate a situation. A woman who cries might also be accused of manipulation, trying to get a man to do what she wants.

Why do children manipulate? To get the parent to do what the child wants or needs. Why do parents manipulate? To get the child to do what the parent wants or needs. When we want someone to do something that she or he might be reluctant to do, we may resort to manipulation if we feel powerless to achieve our needs in another way. But because our cultural double-standard means that we view a child's behavior differently than an adult's, we condemn her behavior and rationalize our own. Challenging our ingrained beliefs about manipulation requires that we simultaneously acknowledge the ways that we as adults use our greater power to manipulate children and also reconsider our judgmental assessment of children's behavior.

We come into the world full of our own power. Systematically, we learn that using our power to speak our truths as children isn't acceptable. As a result, many of us learn to diminish ourselves in order to be accepted and loved by the adults around us. In our disempowerment, we struggle to get our needs met through indirect and "manipulative" means, for which we are judged and even punished. Ultimately, we learn that children are not supposed to try to get their needs met in our culture; we are supposed to accept the care offered us by adults without complaint.

We grow up and, in turn, become parents who are uncomfortable when the children around us use their personal power to get their needs met. We cast ourselves, the adults, as victims of children's manipulations. The powerless (children) become the powerful and we adults, with all our power, see ourselves as the victims of these powerful creatures.

I have certainly fallen into victim mode as a parent. I have to work hard, particularly when I'm under stress, to not feel a sense of powerlessness living with Martel and Greyson and their strong connections to their inner authority and personal power. I was talking with another parent about this sense of powerlessness and was able to trace it back to my own, fairly typical and dysfunctional, childhood. I remembered a time when, as a little girl, I felt powerless to change destructive adult behavior. My anger, fear, and rage were fierce in that moment, and yet they did not change how my parents behaved.

It can be easy to fall back into a sense of powerlessness, to just stay in the feelings of being a victim to children. It takes work to overcome what we learned in our own childhood and to challenge the socialization we have received as truth. To do this, we must look at who in our culture is truly given the power to control and manipulate others.

As adults, we manipulate children in many different ways. Punishment and rewards are ways to manipulate children.[25] For example, if we want a child to try a new vegetable, we might tell her that if she tries it she'll get to eat her dessert or go play. Or we may threaten to take a child home if she doesn't share the swing at the park. We might tell a child to be quiet or she'll be put in time out. Manipulation ranges from quite subtle to overt.

A series of conflicts between Martel and Greyson, then eight and three, reminded me of the power I have to send messages of blame and unworthiness as a way to manipulate. Martel had recently gotten a new video game and was intent on beating all the levels. Because of the level of concentration he needed, he was often frustrated with how loudly Greyson was playing near him.

I felt frustrated with not being able to mediate the situation very effectively. I perceived Martel as inappropriately dominating the family space, despite the fact that Greyson often uses much of the family space to play. I started saying things to Greyson like, "Let's go in the other room before you get Martel angry," or "Martel is getting frustrated, so let's go outside before he yells." Although I said those things to Greyson, my goal was really to get Martel to stop expressing his frustration.

One evening, Martel said that everything that went wrong between him and Greyson that week had been his fault. My not-so-subtle comments had given Martel the clear message that I blamed him for the conflict between him and Greyson. I hadn't needed to say directly to Martel that I thought everything was his fault; he heard it clearly in my manipulative words.

If I am radically honest, I did want Martel to feel some blame in those moments. I wanted him to stop getting angry and frustrated because I was uncomfortable with his reactions. During those times, sometimes Greyson would respond and be upset with Martel and other times he would ignore Martel's comments. Martel's comments triggered me much more than they did Greyson.

Martel's statements made me remember times when I felt I was to blame for everything that went wrong in my house as a child. As a parent, I felt shame and regret for not being able to step back from my triggers and work through my feelings without taking them out on Martel.

As I've learned many times in my relationship with Martel and Greyson, when I'm frustrated or angry I often want them to be responsible for my feelings rather than owning them myself. I use blaming statements or emotion, often out of sheer frustration, in ways that distort the power dynamics between us. I fall back into the idea that I need to manipulate them in order to get what I want.

Manipulation can happen in any number of contexts. Sometimes when I'm being manipulative, it's because I want to stop or encourage a particular behavior. I also have attempted to manipulate the choices Martel and Greyson make in order to ensure that I get the outcome I want. When Martel was two years old, I tried a strategy I had read about in child-rearing books: giving young children two or three choices, all acceptable to the parent, in order to give them the illusion of power and control. I remember feeling good about my ability to "give up" control and "allow" "my" child to make some choices.

I have a very distinct and vivid memory of when Martel called my bluff and challenged the way I was manipulating him. He was about two and a half. After I gave him two choices, he turned to me and said, "That is no choice!".

I jokingly refer to that moment as when I realized he was much smarter than I was. Despite my joking, I struggle to this day with my desire to manipulate Martel and Greyson's choices. My reality is that I struggle with the ways in which I have internalized this paradigm of power and control. Not only did I experience being dominated as a child through the social institutions in our culture, I learned equally well how to wield the tools of domination, including manipulation, with the children in my life.

Another form of manipulation that is challenging to recognize and overcome is the covert control of children's environments to ensure a particular outcome that we as parents have in mind. This manipulation is at the core of alternative mainstream parenting philosophies because it seems kinder than overt control. By filling children's worlds with only the food, toys, media, friends, and activities that we approve of, we do not have to confront the desires and preferences our children may have that would make us uncomfortable.

This desire to manipulate lies under many of the control issues I've struggled with since Martel became a toddler. Before I began to question the appropriateness of controlling Martel, I engaged in this kind of covert manipulation. Rather than be in dialogue with him about what he saw on television, for example, I manipulated what came into the house by choosing not to have cable. Because of my manipulation, he could "freely" choose to watch any PBS Kids shows he wanted.

I constructed a reality for him that made me comfortable. I did the same with food choices, only buying foods I was comfortable with him eating and arranging his life so that he wasn't even aware of many foods I didn't want him to eat.

In reality, I still manipulate the food choices of the family simply because I am the one doing the majority of grocery shopping. But I no longer believe that using power is good and that I have the unquestioned right to exercise it. I now question whether or not I should be manipulating their choices. Admittedly, there are still times when Martel and Greyson ask for some food I consider "junk" and instead I buy an organic brand with which I am more comfortable. Manipulation continues and I continue to question myself.

What am I doing when I manipulate in this covert way? At a fundamental level, I'm limiting and controlling Martel and Greyson so they won't have to—or want to—think for themselves. Manipulation is an attempt to control the ways people think so that they will come to the conclusion that we want them to come to.[26]

By manipulating their choices, I take away the need for Martel and Greyson to think critically about the world around them and the choices they might freely make for themselves. I present a sanitized, constructed version of the world with choices that I am comfortable with, and thus maintain my power over them. I give them the illusion of self-empowerment without losing my own status as the person who controls their lives. I can continue to move them toward the objectives I have chosen for them while feeling self-righteous about my enlightenment.

This kind of manipulation of children by adults reminds me of the movie *The Truman Show*. The movie depicts a reality TV show that has been on the air for 30 years. The main character has no idea that he was born into a town that is in fact a soundstage and that everyone around him is an actor. The weather, the town, and his relationships are all constructed and manipulated by the director. Our manipulation of the surroundings and worlds of children is eerily similar. We create the realities we want for them, rather than trusting them to explore the world around them.

Of course, as parents, we do have an obligation to shield children from legitimate dangers. We help children to understand the danger of cars in the street and sharp knives. We might also choose to not mention opportunities that we genuinely believe would not interest them. But when we filter their access to the world with the intention of creating a certain outcome, we cross the line into manipulation.

Our cultural double-standard means that despite the ways that adults manipulate children, mainstream parenting holds that children must be prevented from manipulating adults. The behavior that we judge to be manipulative in children can take many forms. Often it involves a refusal to accept "no" from an adult. According to mainstream parenting ideals, children should cheerfully accept our refusal to provide them with something they want or need—though of course adults are not expected to accept "no" from a child.

Another behavior often characterized as manipulative is when a child is seen as "testing boundaries." When I hear this phrase, it seems to imply that a child is engaged in a deliberate attempt to provoke an adult, yet I question why we react so negatively to a child exploring the world, including the relationships she has with others, in an attempt to understand how things work. Testing boundaries, again when seen from outside a paradigm of control, is a healthy manifestation of a child's strong desire to learn and understand the world and people around her. When adults do this, we call it *being a scientist*.

Our understanding of children strongly affects our perception of their behavior. If we view children as needing to be controlled and tamed, then we'll see their behavior as manipulative and seek to control it. When we view children and their behavior without the frame of reference of control parenting, we can see that their "manipulation" is a manifestation of the lack of power children have to effect the change they need in their lives and to get their needs met. Viewing the behavior as expressing a legitimate need, we can begin to consider how we might meet that need. As children begin to trust that their needs will be met and as they grow and mature, we can trust that the way they communicate their needs will also mature. By meeting the needs of children, no matter how they communicate those needs to us, we are not reinforcing the "bad" behavior, we are reinforcing the message that children deserve to be treated with respect and that their needs are legitimate.

Rather than condemning a child for manipulation, perhaps we need to look at the reasons why this manipulation occurs. Perhaps our children manipulate because we've taught them how to manipulate others through our own example. Perhaps it happens because the child feels so powerless that she has no other options. When I am in victim mode, perceiving myself to be powerless, I resort to manipulation. Perhaps children are only doing the same in trying to get their own needs met.

Learning

In the first three years of life, children are able to learn a complex set of skills. They learn to walk and talk, and even to do these at the same time. Young children display an amazing curiosity and a drive to explore and learn as much as they can about the world around them.

Once a child moves past three years old, our dominant mainstream culture begins to question her ability to learn on her own. We believe that we must begin to control a child's learning process to ensure that she becomes "well-educated." Sending a child to school is a given in our society. Although we've questioned the effectiveness of our schools and have instituted a number of reform measures on local, regional, and national levels, we often don't consider alternatives to school or question the right of parents to make a unilateral choice to force a child to go to school in order to learn. School can be a legitimate and positive choice for some children. It may not be the right choice for all children.

When Martel was old enough for kindergarten, we decided, rather than sending him to school, to create an environment where he has access to a wide range of information, experiences, and people. In addition, we have been willing facilitators to his learning process when he needs help, such as looking up information or offering opportunities to pursue his interests.[27] Embracing this natural and experiential learning process has been an opportunity for me to challenge my notions about teaching, learning, and what it means to be educated.

I believe based on my experiences as a teacher, university administrator, and adult learner that there are a wide variety of ways that we can learn and that learning is not confined to the classroom or school. In my professional career, I taught undergraduates in a variety of settings: in the classroom, through workshops, in dialogue, and in one-on-one interactions. I viewed my role as an educator, but also as a facilitator. I witnessed learning occur both in and outside the classroom. Based on my experiences as a learner and an educator, experiential learning—learning that is connected to students' real lives—is more effective than a top-down educational process.

Universities and other educational institutions can foster experiential learning, but it occurs naturally and continually as children—and adults—interact with their worlds. As a parent, I have had the opportunity to watch both Martel and Greyson learn from the minute they were born. Without instruction from me, they learned to feed themselves, walk, and talk. They learned how to manipulate objects and their environment. They learned how to run and yell at the same time.

Martel, being older than Greyson, has also learned many of the skills and information he would have been exposed to in school. He learned to read without formal instruction through his interactions with the computer, video games, trading cards, and books, as well as by asking us questions. He has learned a great deal of math through video games and he went through a period where he loved to have me give him math problems. I have no doubt that both he and Greyson will continue to learn joyfully and without coercion.

Although the initial decision to homeschool was made by us as parents, we occasionally ask Martel and Greyson whether they would like to go to school. Thus far, they have chosen to continue homeschooling. However, I would also support Martel and Greyson if they choose to go to school. For me, what is important is that they have the opportunity to choose. I am not anti-school; I am against forcing a child to fit into a one-size-fits-all educational model if that model doesn't best serve her needs.

School dominates the lives of most children from age four or five to 18. School controls their daily and seasonal schedules, requires them to accept authority figures with little or no choice, and imposes requirements on what they do and even think about during much of their time.

Beyond these obvious controls, schools enshrine and perpetuate beliefs about children as less than adults and may even limit what children believe they can become. The effects of school experiences inevitably reach into adulthood—not only in the intended sense of providing an education to prepare children for adult responsibilities, but also in unintended, sometimes damaging ways.

Just as it is important for us to question our control over children's emotional expressions, bodies, and food, we need to question the kind of institutional control school imposes on children and how we can help children deal with that level of control if they choose the option of attending school. We must understand the way schools by their very nature disempower children, place conditions on their ability to have their needs met, and perpetuate the paradigm of control and power.

All educational institutions are based, to greater or lesser degrees, on relationships of control. Teachers, in our dominant culture, are set up to exert power and control in the classroom. The position of teacher is believed to carry with it a particular kind of authority that includes having special knowledge that should be passed on to children as well as the power of the institution to enforce behavioral norms.

Arguably, this power is tenuous at times, particularly as children grow older and seek to create a classroom culture that better fits their notions of how they should be treated. And many individual teachers work to mitigate the imbalance of power and control in the classroom. However, because teachers are themselves controlled by the hierarchy above them, their scope for empowering children is limited.

In considering the power of the school system, educational reform advocate John Holt[28] compared it to "a kind of jail":

> Children are subject peoples. School for them is a kind of jail. Do they not, to some extent, escape and frustrate the relentless, insatiable pressure of their elders by withdrawing the most intelligent and creative parts of their minds from the scene? Is this not at least a partial explanation of the

extraordinary stupidity that otherwise bright children so often show in school? The stubborn and dogged "I don't get it" with which they meet the instructions and explanations of their teachers—may it not be a statement of resistance as well as one of panic and flight?[29]

Schools use their control over children to drive performance. As babies and children who grow up within the paradigm that embraces power and control over others, we learn that we must please our parents in order to maintain their love and acceptance. Teachers soon take over the role and authority of parents, and the majority of students—who are not motivated by an intrinsic desire to learn whatever material the curriculum requires of them at the time—learn to perform to please their teachers and parents in order to get some of their emotional needs met. Alternatively, they may choose not to perform and suffer the consequences of not meeting the expectations of parents and teachers.

Holt questioned early in his career the pressure of forced performance:

> After all I have said about the need for keeping children under pressure, I find myself coming to realize that what hampers their thinking, what drives them into these narrow and defensive strategies, is a feeling that they must please the grownups at all costs. The really able thinkers in our class turn out to be, without exception, children who don't feel strongly the need to please the grownups. Some of them are good students, some not so good; but good or not, they don't work to please us, but to please themselves.[30]

At the core of required performance is fear.[31] If we don't perform adequately to meet the expectations of others, we fear losing love, respect, humane treatment, and dignity, among other things. When this fear is part of our daily lives at home, at school, or at work, we move into survival mode and leave our best selves behind. Holt described this process based on his observations:

> What I now see for the first time is the mechanism by which fear destroys intelligence, the way it affects a child's whole way of looking at, thinking about, and dealing with life....Like good soldiers, they control their fears, live with them, and adjust themselves to them. But the trouble is, and here is a vital difference between school and war, the adjustments children make to their fears are almost wholly bad, destructive of their intelligence and capacity....[T]he scared learner is always a poor learner.[32]

The performance needed to be successful in school goes beyond the expectations of teachers, grades, and standardized tests. Certainly those are measures of "success" in institutionalized schooling, but the need to perform carries over into the relationships between the individuals within the system. Peers, teachers, parents, and administrators all require a particular kind of performance in order to grant approval and acceptance.

We are, in essence, a society that is conditional. Acceptance by the dominant culture is conditioned upon adherence to the rules established by that culture. We participate in our own disempowerment as individuals by believing and perpetuating the idea that we must perform in order to be successful.

Our society's performance norms come at a high price for almost everyone involved. We may bend to outer authority, even when it violates our inner authority. We may lose touch with our authentic selves because we have bought into the cultural norm of fitting in to be successful (as defined by the culture) and accepted.

As parents, we pass on the teachings of this dominant paradigm when we require our children to perform. When a child exercises the fundamental right to be who she is, she is punished if who she is isn't what society or adults want for her. We label the child as difficult or rebellious. As adults, when we experience the defiance of a child to meeting the expectations that are set for her, we may be triggered, experiencing emotions that have more to do with our own history and baggage than with the actual present issue with the child.

In that moment, we may be re-experiencing the feelings of disempowerment and anger of our own childhood. Perhaps we were expected to perform no matter how we felt and we expect the same from others around us. Rather than questioning whether or not this performance expectation is reasonable, we might choose to do what was done to us as children.

In order to protect the status quo, our institutions and systems need individuals who are willing to adhere to performance standards. These performance requirements are about productivity and conformity rather than growth, creativity, and learning.

Standardization serves institutions, not individuals. Not meeting the expectations of institutionalized education results in labeling. As another advocate for educational reform, John Taylor Gatto[33], argues:

Children need the widest possible range of roads in order to find the right one to accommodate themselves. The premise upon which mass compulsion schooling is based is dead wrong. It tries to shoehorn every style, culture, and personality into one ugly boot that fits nobody.[34]

So schools enforce performance and conformity not to support learning but rather to meet their own institutional needs. In the same way, schools are among the primary institutions that reinforce power-over dynamics. As Gatto points out:

Each day, schools reinforce how absolute and arbitrary power really is by granting and denying access to fundamental needs for toilets, water, privacy and movement. In this way, basic human rights which usually require only individual volition, are transformed into privileges not to be taken for granted.[35]

Four decades before Gatto, Holt wrote, "What [teachers and schools] prize above all is docility, suggestibility; the child who will do what he is told; or even better, the child who will do what is wanted without even having to be told."[36]

School teaches us what we need to do in order to perform as adults in the work environment. We learn what it means to be told what to do and to have our performance evaluated by those who have more power. Our external behavior is judged by those around us. We learn that there are written and unwritten rules about how we should act.

It is a mistake to assume that institutionalized schooling is primarily about learning facts or skills. In fact, it was designed to meet the needs of the larger industrialized world in which compulsory schooling was developed in the early 1900's.[37] The first mission statement of Rockefeller's General Education Board, published in 1912 as an essay, describes the dream of the architects of forced schooling.

> In our dream...people yield themselves with perfect docility to our molding hands. The present educational conventions [intellectual and character education] fade from our minds, and...we work our own good will upon a grateful and responsive folk. We shall not try to make these people or any of their children into philosophers or men of learning or men of science. We have not to raise up from among them authors, educators, poets or men of letters. We shall not search for embryo great artists, painters, musicians, lawyers, doctors, preachers, politicians, statesmen of whom we have ample supply. The task we set before ourselves is a very simple as well as very beautiful one...we will organize our children...and teach them to do in a perfect way the things their fathers and mothers are doing in an imperfect way.[38]

We may be shocked by this today and want to believe that schools are no longer focused on this "dream," yet the systems established by that General Education Board persist today with little structural change.

In writing about the problems of our educational system I want to challenge our assumptions about how and where learning occurs. A belief that learning can only occur in the classroom limits the possibilities for our children and ourselves. If we choose to accept all aspects of school without question, we discourage our children from being able to critically examine their own experiences and learning.

For all of its problems, school may offer resources that a child may wish to access. If she does freely choose school, we can still ensure that her home environment is supportive and respectful of her decision without recreating the control paradigm inherent in school systems. Parents do not have to stand in proxy for teachers and the system by rewarding and punishing homework completion and grades. Instead, we can support whatever level the child chooses to achieve in school by rejecting the role of school proxy. We can create a place of safety and caring within the home environment that offsets the experiences that might be harmful or challenging in her school environment. We can encourage her to remain authentic and connected to her own inner authority even as she chooses school.

It can be a challenge to trust in the ability of children to learn without being taught by an authority figure. We may trust children when they are very young, but then we receive the message that they must be turned over to experts in order to continue learning. We accept the right of those experts to control the content, the timing, and the methods by which a child learns. Often, we accept even the need for an expert, believing that we are not ourselves qualified to guide our children. We hand our authority over to others in spite of what we may have observed in our children in the first few years of their lives.

Challenging these assumptions about the nature of learning can be difficult because we are taught that children will not learn unless they are forced. Just as in other realms of their lives, it's the coercion and control of a child's learning process that turns her away from her natural desire to learn more about the world. We then decide, because she doesn't show sufficient motivation, that she must be controlled even further. We create another vicious cycle

of control that in the end hurts the child even while it fails to meet
our intent of helping her learn.

The examples I've offered in this chapter are just a few of the ways
that children's lives are routinely and thoughtlessly controlled. You
will be able to identify many other ways that adults control
children. Once we begin to recognize the pervasiveness of the
control paradigm and the resulting cycle of control, we can then
become aware of how it operates in more and more areas of our
lives, not just in our role as parents.

Recognizing this pervasiveness of control and domination is a
critical first step towards letting go and liberating children and
ourselves. In Chapter 3, we'll take a step back to look at more
research into control parenting versus supportive parenting and in
Chapter 4 we'll discuss taking steps toward liberation and freedom.

CHAPTER THREE

Controlling Parenting versus Supportive Parenting

A S A PARENT, it can be terrifying to think about letting go of control. It may be necessary to face some deeply entrenched beliefs and fears. Especially if we had little control over our lives as children, we may have even more difficulty letting go as adults. We often spend our childhoods waiting for our turn to take the reins and follow our own paths. And now, I'm asking you to think about letting go of controlling.

In order to make an informed decision about whether to reject or perpetuate the paradigm of control, let's examine what recent research tells us about what control really does to children and how it impacts them beyond childhood. Then we'll look at what research says about the effects of supportive parenting.

The Problems of Control

Because we have been socialized to believe that control is necessary, we can ignore the harm that control does to children. We may choose to see the negative aspects of control as the lesser of two evils; if we were to let go of control, we believe we would experience chaos and our children would grow into dysfunctional adults. Thus, we're willing to exercise control and domination, because we believe that the negative feelings children experience when they are being controlled are better than the alternative.

Within the paradigm of control, when children are "out of control" it seems logical that parents need to impose more control so that children can eventually learn self-control. Recent research, however, actually tells us the opposite. Studies of control parenting in general and of particular controlling behaviors such as conditional approval all demonstrate the damage inflicted on children by the paradigm of control.

For example, it turns out that there is a direct relationship between interpersonal control (one person controlling another) and a higher tendency toward violence.[1] If I feel as though someone is trying to control me, I am more likely to feel dehumanized and I am more likely to respond with violence. Again we see how the vicious cycle of control is perpetuated: the adult attempts to control an "out of control" child, the child responds with resistance or violence, which reaffirms for the adult that the child needs to be controlled.

Studies of adolescents' perceptions of control by parents have consistently found that psychological control—parents manipulating, invalidating, and constraining children's psychological and emotional experiences and expressions—was related to higher levels of behavioral and emotional problems.[2] Also, withdrawal of love or affection and parental neglect result in a child who is more likely to have a negative self-image.[3]

As mentioned in the section on food, control and coercion actually diminish a child's ability to self-regulate. When we pressure a child to eat healthy foods, we get results for a short time, but we ultimately reduce her preferences for such food. Even offering nutritional information can negatively affect a child's pattern of food acceptance.[4]

All humans have a need for autonomy, to feel free from control by others.[5] When the need for autonomy is frustrated by our parents, we are likely to feel more anxiety and anger and to focus on our own frustrations and inability to cope. When we feel obligated or controlled we also are less likely to feel empathy and caring towards others.[6]

Controlling parenting is even harmful when parents have other, more positive parenting behaviors as well.[7] We cannot make up for our controlling behavior through other positive choices. The results of this particular line of research are striking. We can tell a child how much we love her, we can be highly responsive to her distress—and yet our choice to control her will still be harmful to her emotional and psychological well-being.

One of the very powerful ways we try to control children, one I've certainly used, is conditional approval and love. If Martel or Greyson does something that I approve of, I might praise him or demonstrate positive feelings towards him. If he does something that I disapprove of, I may move away from him or somehow communicate that he is not a "good boy."

All babies and children need to feel positive regard by their parents. They desire love and need protection. We as parents may feel that no matter what, we'll always love the children who share our lives, and we may also believe that they know and understand this love. But when we condition love and approval on certain behavior or expressions, children may begin to believe that their self-worth is based on our approval. Certainly they believe that our positive regard in that moment is dependent on our approval of their behavior—after all, that's the point of conditional approval.

As a result, children become externally motivated, depending on outside approval. They lose the internal motivation that comes from being connected to their inner authority. Studies show that disconnection from inner authority and motivation, and the orientation toward external motivation that goes with it, is likely to lead to lower self-worth, destructive behavior, lack of trust in their own judgment, and overall lower mental health.[8]

After becoming externally motivated, a child who grows up with conditional approval and control exerted by others may actually internalize these experiences and begin to exert conditional approval on herself even without a parent or teacher being there. This internalized control diminishes feelings of autonomy and freedom to choose her own actions, resulting in less happiness.[9] Many adults have the experience of "hearing" a disapproving parent's voice when they do something that would not have been approved of during their childhood.

As a result of our conditional approval, we may believe we've taught a child self-control. When we remove our cultural blinders, we can instead see that we've used our conditional love to force her to choose between her own intuition or inner authority and another more powerful person's authority. She may be "playing the game," behaving in our presence as though she has bought into our ideas, or she may in fact have lost her inner authority and replaced it with an authority not her own. John Holt observed this phenomenon and commented, "How much easier her life would be if we did not continually oblige her to choose between our adult approval and her self-respect."[10]

As she continues to grow, we may observe with dismay that she chooses to substitute the power of her peer group over her own inner authority. Yet this is the logical outcome of our own behavior. We have taught her, through our own actions, that those who have the power to withdraw their love and approval need to be followed. If, at that point in her life, the approval of her peer group is more important than that of her parents, she will likely choose her peers.[11]

Not only do we exert interpersonal control over children, we can also enforce cultural norms that are harmful to children. As parents, we stand in proxy for the larger system, which, in order to continue to exist, must deny personal power and authority and impose systemic and institutional power and authority.

One quite striking example of systemic power and the ways in which individuals represent the system to enforce social norms is gender identity socialization. From even before birth, we feel a need to identify a baby's gender. We assign blue for boys and pink for girls. We announce the birth of a baby with "It's a boy!" or "It's a girl!". We feel that boys must learn to be tough and strong and girls must learn to nurture and take care of others.

Even if we don't consciously agree with these norms, our lifelong enculturation and the powerful cultural messages all around us make it likely that we will inadvertently perpetuate these ideas. Through children's books, clothing, songs, games, and a myriad of cultural messages, we teach children their proper place and behavior based on their genitalia.

If a boy wants to play with dolls, wears pink, or cries, our society's gender norms are called into question and challenged. Individuals who believe in these gender norms, or who do not question them, are likely to reinforce those norms through teasing, withholding love, scolding, or punishment. Even seemingly gentle redirection, such as suggesting that he choose different clothes or toys, furthers the message that he must conform to the culture's norms. If the boy has been disconnected from his inner authority and has no support to follow his own path, he has little internal guidance to help him withstand the pressure to conform.

Ultimately, control and domination of children disconnects them from their inner authority. If, instead, they are allowed to maintain a strong connection to their inner authority and personal power, peers and social institutions are less able to influence their conditioning and learning. Instead of accepting as truth anything given to them by authority figures, they are able to critically examine what's happening around them. Supportive and respectful parenting is critical to maintaining this strong connection.

Maintaining our connection to inner authority is in many respects a subversive act. By resisting the automatic replacement of our own authority with that of adults, institutions, and systems, we begin to break the cycle of socialization. This subversion, however, doesn't mean that we become lawless, nor does it mean that we become social outcasts.

Subversion and resisting authority are sometimes mistakenly associated with anarchy and chaos, but that is not what I am advocating. What I am advocating is a rejection of the ways in which we normalize domination and control of children and other less-powerful groups in our society. Without resistance, we absorb the paradigm of control. Domination becomes a commonsense, everyday behavior, and we lose sight of how we willingly reinforce control relationships in our day-to-day actions.[12]

Despite the cultural norms that advocate control as a necessary parenting tool, research tells us a different story. Controlling parenting results in

- feelings of dehumanization and a higher tendency toward violence;
- higher levels of behavioral and emotional problems;
- negative self-image;
- diminishment of a child's ability to self-regulate food intake;
- being less likely to feel empathy and caring towards others; and
- external motivation that results in lower self-worth, destructive behavior, lack of trust in their own judgment, and overall lower mental health.

The good news is we can choose to parent differently and the research on supportive parenting shows the positive impacts of moving out of the control paradigm.

The Impact of Supportive Parenting

In turning away from a paradigm of control, supportive parenting provides a way for us to affirm the dignity and humanity of children. We acknowledge that children have vulnerabilities and need support, but these vulnerabilities don't diminish their right to be treated and acknowledged as competent human beings who have the ability to learn and grow without being controlled.

Through supportive parenting we can come to our relationships with children from a place of mutuality. We can work to equalize the power differentials inherent in a social structure that is based on power-over dynamics. We can respect and learn from each other, acknowledging and even celebrating the differences in our experiences and knowledge.

Supportive parenting meets children's needs. It creates a foundation from which they can move out into the world knowing that they're loved and accepted for who they are. They go out from our care knowing that they can be trusted and that they are competent to handle what will come their way. Their emotional reserves are full. They don't have to struggle to get their voices heard and they believe their needs and desires are important. Depending on their age, they may also have the ability to empathize with others.

We've talked extensively about control parenting. Before we examine the research about supportive parenting, let's consider what this different approach to parenting might look like.

Supportive parenting can take different forms. It can be the emotional support that results in a child or adolescent feeling cared for and loved. When our teen is struggling with the emotional fallout from a relationship, for example, listening, accepting her feelings, and allowing her to process her experiences without judgment provides her with the support she needs. Listening to a child vent her emotions about why a particular incident was unfair, without trying to force her to see a different point of view in the moment, is another form of emotional support.

Other forms of support may be practical and financial, helping with the tasks that children and adolescents want to accomplish. Of course, our ability to provide financial support is dependent on the family's overall situation, but parents can provide practical help to a child trying to achieve a particular goal or objective. Helping a child find a way to earn her own money—without coercion or pressure from a parent—might be one model of practical support. Taking a child's wishes seriously, even when fulfilling them is not immediately achievable, can also be a form of support.

Supportive parents can provide information that might be geared toward solving a particular problem. For example, parents can facilitate a child's interest in learning a particular skill or knowledge base by connecting the child to another person with appropriate expertise. For a child who is struggling with a problem that has come up with a friend, supportive parenting can be as simple as asking whether or not she wants help. If she does want help, parent and child can work together to think of possible ways to resolve the problem. In this case, it is important that the parent not impose a solution, but rather give support and space to the child to find her best solution.

Facilitating a child's need or desire for information can be challenging, since children may not be ready for or comfortable with all the information available on a topic. As Martel and Greyson grow older and their worlds naturally expand, they're exposed to more ideas, people, and experiences. My role as a supportive and respectful parent is to facilitate their process of exploration, to be their partner in the journey. To simultaneously support their desire for information and their personal boundaries, I have learned to give them a preview of information they might be asking for.

For example, Martel went through a period when he was eight of watching shows (which we watched together) that had sexual jokes and innuendos. He would often ask me what certain words meant. At first, I would just give him the answer, and he discovered that some of my answers made him uncomfortable. We talked about it and agreed that if a word he asked me about had to do with sex, I would tell him that and he would decide if he wanted to know the details. I wasn't withholding or controlling information, but giving him control over whether or not he was ready to hear the information.

Traditional mainstream parenting might view my allowing Martel to watch a show with any kind of sexual content as irresponsible. My giving up control in this case, though, wasn't an abdication of responsibility. In fact, we've communicated openly about the kinds and levels of information Martel feels he's ready for. Rather than his boundaries being my decision, he can determine them himself with my support. We're involved and connected. This is the heart of supportive parenting: replacing control with involvement and connection to facilitate children's needs and their journey through childhood.

While supportive parenting is focused on meeting children's needs, it does not disregard the needs of parents or institutions like schools or workplaces. The fear that children parented without arbitrary controls will be wild and uncooperative and grow into self-centered, dysfunctional adults is unfounded. In fact, evidence tells us just the opposite.

We've seen that control creates the opposite effect of what parents intend. On the other hand, research shows that children are more likely to adopt supportive behaviors with others when they experience supportive parenting.

Children who grow up in supportive families have parents who are responsive to their needs, emotionally involved, and interested in their lives. A large variety of studies have shown that these children are less likely to develop low self-esteem, depression, and aggression as adolescents.[13] If we consistently nurture and support children, they believe that they're trustworthy as well as competent and likable.[14]

Psychologists have studied the characteristics of well-being and found that for healthy functioning, adults and children must satisfy their needs for:

- self-determination
- autonomy
- control of their own decisions and actions
- competence
- supportive companionship
- respect
- the opportunity to nurture others
- being nurtured by others

Finally, a baby or child needs to be positively regarded by those who are most significant to her.[15] These studies show that a child needs supportive parents, not coercion and control, in order to be a healthy child and a healthy adult.

Although supportive parenting provides for all of the needs listed above, its role in fostering autonomy deserves special mention. As parents, we play a large role in fostering an environment that allows for autonomy by letting go of control.

The more autonomy we feel, the more human we feel and the less likely we are to resort to violence.[16] Autonomy is characterized by a feeling of being free. People are happier and healthier when they feel autonomous.[17] This sense of well-being is maximized when young people behave in a way that's consistent with their internal values and wishes, as opposed to the values and wishes of others.[18] Support for autonomy also promotes empathy. When our need for autonomy is satisfied we're more likely to feel positive.[19]

We might question whether autonomy is seen as a value only in more individualistic cultures such as the United States and many western countries, as opposed to collectivistic cultures like those in many Asian countries. Cross-cultural research finds that adolescents whose parents give them freedom in decision-making and are supportive, warm, and loving report more motivation in school and higher levels of well-being regardless of whether the culture is individualistic or collectivistic.[20] In a comparison of parents and youth in China and the United States, the impact of control on the psychological functioning of children was negative in both cultures.[21]

Despite all the benefits of supportive parenting, however, as we challenge ourselves to treat children with the same level of respect we offer to adults we begin to see that this is more than an issue of achieving positive outcomes. We shouldn't treat children with respect and affirm their dignity and humanity just because we want respectful, caring adults—although it is true that this is the likely result. If our intent in establishing respectful relationships is merely to manipulate children to become what we want, then we're still operating from a place of control.

We should treat children with the respect that all human beings deserve simply because it is the right thing to do. How we treat others in our lives is a reflection of our own humanity. If the children in our lives experience control, domination, and oppression as a result of their status as children, we all lose as human beings.

The freedom of children is tied to our freedom as well. When children have the freedom to develop their inner authority and stay connected to their authentic selves, they become fuller human beings. We, as parents, grow as well when we abandon mainstream society's expectation that we treat children with mistrust and disrespect. We regain what we lost in our own childhood.

Often the disempowerment we experienced as children was coupled with the promise of control when we grew up. "When you're an adult...," "when you're the mom...," and "when you have your own house..." are things many of us heard. To give up our turn to take control now, when we were promised that we could make the rules, may be very difficult.

By giving up on our "turn," though, we are also giving up on perpetuating the paradigm of control, and thus we give a gift to our children and our society. The other reality of giving up our turn is that the chapter of our lives that we spend with children at home is really quite short; all too soon we will get to control what goes on in our houses without having to coerce those who are less powerful than we are.

Letting go of control does not mean that we never say "no." One reality of life is that we don't have the ability to expose children to all the possibilities available in our complex and wide-ranging world. I physically and financially don't have the ability to bring home every type of food possible for Greyson and Martel to try. However, the natural limits of our world are not the same as controls imposed by parents. They aren't arbitrary decisions, but simply the reality of our life. At the same time, we must not let these realities limit our thinking or become an excuse for not taking children's wishes seriously. Perhaps, if we move beyond automatic patterns of thought and behavior, we may see different possibilities.

A New View of Childhood

If I go back to my own early experience as a parent, I engaged in control and domination from a belief that my control was necessary to ensure that Martel and Greyson would be able to interact in ways that would help them successfully navigate the world (both as children and as adults). I had internalized a view of children as adults-in-training and thought this was my responsibility as a parent. Despite the common belief that control is necessary to a child's development into a socially competent adult, we've discovered that it is not only unnecessary, but in fact counterproductive.

As parents letting go of control, we can often struggle with how to care for children and help meet their needs without controlling them. The balance of providing care without moving into control can be challenging, especially when we believe that a child's health might be at stake. With food, media access, or issues of personal hygiene, our fears about future negative outcomes if children make choices that we don't agree with can be hard to overcome.

Letting go of control doesn't mean we abdicate our responsibility to care for the children in our lives. My goal is for us, as parents, to critically examine what we're afraid of. Through this process of self-examination we can ask ourselves questions that challenge our automatic thoughts and reactions. Is it really true that if a child eats sugar, I'm setting her up to be obese and unhealthy? If I don't teach a child to say "thank you," do I really know that she will become a rude and impolite person? Do I really know that whatever behavior I dislike in a child today will result in negative outcomes in the future?

If fear about bad things happening to children in the future is our motivator for the actions we take, we can easily slip from caring for children to controlling them. When we control others and operate out of fear, we're less connected and less respectful, and love is diminished.

I advocate for liberating ourselves from this paradigm of control and domination because it fundamentally limits our potential as human beings. Our choices are narrowed when we are afraid and when we believe that people should behave only in certain prescribed ways. Our creativity is limited and our capacity for growth and learning is stunted.

If we can abandon the idea that children are adults-in-training, we can also move beyond the desire to control their behaviors out of fear. The new view of children and childhood that many sociologists began to explore at the end of the 20th century was the idea that children are competent social beings, though different from adults. When researchers began to closely examine children's behavior from this perspective they found that children operated from a nuanced and subtle understanding of social relationships and social ordering. Socialization is taking place in children, but it's because they are already competent social beings that they have the ability to be socialized.[22]

This new view of children and childhood also looks at the traditional adult-child relationship as a social construction that serves the broader social system of inequality and creates unequal relationships between adults and children. The belief that children are adults-in-training necessitates that adults have power and control over children in order to ensure proper socialization.[23] But if we see children as competent in their own right, our responsibility becomes focused on how we can care for—rather than control—them. Our relationships are recast in a more mutual paradigm, a partnership in which we can learn from each other while attending to children's unique needs from a place of respect.

This change in how we view children also shifts the ways we view their behavior. If children are merely adults-in-training, we see them as reckless and at risk, and we may disapprove of their behavior. If we believe that children aren't able to reason and are incompetent, then we more easily reject their ideas and thought processes. Acting from these stereotypes, especially when they operate outside of our conscious thought processes—as stereotypes generally do—can create or worsen tension and conflict and increase mistrust.[24]

If, instead, we see children as the competent and complex human beings that they are, we can begin to see their behavior beyond the polarity of negative and positive. We can begin to see the nuances of who they are and how they see the world. Our role becomes that of a facilitator. We help them to access the world in the ways they desire, while providing information as needed—all the while learning with them.

A strategy I have encountered that is useful in visualizing this new way of being with children is to imagine that children are beloved adult visitors from another country who don't know our customs or ways. How would we treat such a visitor? We would give them guidance and support without shame or judgment. We would accept their mistakes, celebrate their accomplishments with them, and cherish the experience of being with them as they explored and gained mastery of our culture. This is how life can be with children when we let go of our fears and control.

The research is clear. Controlling parenting, despite its mainstream acceptance, damages children even as it fails to achieve the very goals on which it is allegedly focused. We must actively and resoundingly reject controlling parenting in spite of the cultural pressure we may face.

Supportive parenting, on the other hand, is likely to produce healthy adults and, more important, is ethically right. Through the process of supportive parenting we have the opportunity to create a space that invites children to explore themselves and the world around them from a foundation of love and support, rather than fear and control.

The belief that we can form mutual relationships across our identities of adult and child embraces a belief that if one group in our society is limited, we all lose out. Society as a whole loses the potential of the individuals who are boxed in, while the impact to the individuals is even more severe. Therefore, as supportively-parented children grow, they can reshape and enhance our society as a whole.

Even if we know the value and believe in the ethics of support-ive parenting, it can be difficult to move out of a belief that children must experience control by adults and institutions in order to develop into the kind of adults that are able to function in our society. To reject control as a dominant frame of reference and a necessary parenting tool will require us to create a different vision for the child-parent relationship. Because most of us didn't experience a relationship based on respect for our competencies and abilities as children, we have few models for how these relationships can develop and flourish. In the next chapter, we'll talk about the first steps toward liberating ourselves from a paradigm of control and domination.

CHAPTER FOUR

Steps Toward
Liberation and Freedom

THE REALIZATION THAT we have been operating from a paradigm of control and domination may come to us gradually or it may come through one or more critical incidents that expose our behavior for what it truly is. Changing our behavior, on the other hand, is sure to be a slow process. We must unlearn much of what we know about children and parenting, and relearn how to create a relationship with children from a foundation of mutuality and trust. We have the "a ha!" moments and then we have to try to integrate our new awareness into our daily lives.

In this chapter I address the ways we move toward freedom from control and domination. In the first section, I provide a different perspective on the role of rebellion and how it might move us toward liberation as parents and, as a result, the liberation of the children who rebel against our control. I then discuss the need to liberate ourselves and develop a liberatory consciousness—an awareness of domination and freedom and a conscious commitment to the liberation of others.

In Chapter 5, we'll move on to specific strategies and tools for unlearning and relearning and discuss how to create and sustain the change we desire within ourselves.

Rebellion and Freedom

Rebellion by children, when viewed through the lens of adult control and domination, carries negative connotations and consequences. According to mainstream philosophy, a child must learn how to fit into the systems we create and sustain, such as institutionalized child-care, institutionalized education, and the workforce. Though we love the children in our lives, we're taught to see them as less than full human beings and we subject them to control "for their own good." What this control really benefits, however, is not our children but our social institutions.

If, as parents, we are immersed in this power and control dynamic, we view rebellion by children as a problem. When children rebel against adult control and the psychological or physical violence of control and domination, they're cast as disaffected, violent, uncontrollable, and defiant. Because we've normalized our control, it's the children and youth who, when reacting, become the subject of our scrutiny, rather than our own behavior.

However, the rebellion of children can also be viewed as feedback. Rebellion is a clear message that we have attempted to control a child in a way she will not accept. When we discover she'll no longer go along with being controlled, we have the opportunity to go inward to examine our behavior as parents. In this way, rebellion can be the first step in the liberation process.

Children rebel against adult oppression in various ways. In my own case, Martel lashed out at others around him who didn't have a lot of power, like other children. He couldn't rebel against me directly for fear of losing love and approval. His anger was both outwardly directed at others and inwardly directed at himself. As Martel's rebellion continued against my refusal to treat him with the kind of respect that should be afforded any human being, I began to question more and more what my role was.

I came to see Martel's rebellion against my controls as a gift. In fact, rebellion is a process in which the dominated restore the humanity of the dominator. As educational philosopher Paulo Freire wrote:

> Yet it is—paradoxical though it may seem—precisely in the response of the oppressed to the violence of their oppressors that a gesture of love may be found. ... Whereas the violence of the oppressors prevents the oppressed from being fully human, the response of the latter to this violence is grounded in the desire to pursue the right to be human. As the oppressors dehumanize others and violate their rights, they themselves also become dehumanized. As the oppressed, fighting to be human, take away the oppressors' power to dominate and suppress, they restore to the oppressors the humanity they had lost in the exercise of oppression.[1]

Martel very clearly had the need to be treated and respected as fully human. The more I denied him his humanity, the more he pushed back. Ultimately, his acts of rebellion did restore my own humanity. I began to see in him the things that I had been denied as a child.

At times, this ongoing process can be incredibly difficult. I feel as though my own childhood was lost to the systems in place at the time I was born, and I struggle with the impulse to lash out and place myself in the role of victim.

Being a parent opens up our core in ways that can be deeply uncomfortable. Because of Martel's rebellion, I've been able to reflect on my worldview and attitudes about children and have begun to liberate myself while working to create a liberating environment in the family.

The rebellion of children presents us with a choice: will we focus on the child's behavior and silence her cry for respectful treatment? Or will we accept the invitation to investigate the source of the rebellion?

Liberation and Liberatory Consciousness

The process of liberating ourselves and the children in our lives from a paradigm of domination and control usually begins with an incident that creates discomfort and results in cognitive dissonance.[2] Cognitive dissonance occurs when we try to hold two conflicting ideas within our minds.

In my own case, I had invested a lot of energy into my identity as an individual and a leader committed to justice, freedom, and growth. Not only did I believe my professional work reflected this commitment, I also thought as a parent I was committed to this.

Through a series of critical incidents, such as Martel's increasing anger and rebellion, the need to decide whether or not Martel would go to school, and watching the video of myself treating Martel with disrespect, I experienced profound cognitive dissonance because my actions were not consistent with what I believed about myself. The descriptions I read about dominating and controlling parents were more consistent with my behavior than my ideals. The person I saw in the mirror was not the person I wanted to be. I was a hypocrite. Throughout my adult life, I had challenged hypocrisy. Now it was time to go to work on myself.

We can use the discomfort of cognitive dissonance as another opportunity to move inward and challenge ourselves to reflect on our behaviors, values, and beliefs. When I began to understand the ways my behavior as a parent were controlling and disrespectful, I started the process of unlearning my socialization and in its place learning new ways of being with Martel and Greyson.

I see this learning process as a spiral.[3] While institutionalized learning tends to be linear, with one concept building directly on another, experiential, lifelong learning can be visualized in a spiral pattern, in which ideas and issues are revisited again and again. As the spiral widens, more experience and knowledge is brought to bear, and our understanding and competence deepens.

The spiral imagery reflects the never-ending nature of organic learning; we're always adding new experiences that affect how we view a particular issue. It's also, for me, a comforting image because I can acknowledge that I'm always learning. If I fall back into old behaviors, I have the opportunity to add new knowledge and continue to learn. It gives me hope that I can eventually change my harmful behaviors and beliefs.

With regard to my experiences as a parent, the learning spiral incorporates the process by which:

- I have some experience, whether positive or negative;
- I reflect on that experience and my actions, as well as the impact and results of my actions;

- I think about how I might generalize my experience more broadly in my relationships; and
- I apply new action to subsequent experiences.

This process of action and reflection is called praxis, and although it sounds lengthy and mechanistic it can happen quickly and naturally. I'm often acting and reflecting simultaneously, adjusting my actions as I go along.

In the liberation process we begin to understand the true nature of how power, control, and oppression operate individually and systemically.[4] But we still live within the dynamic of power and control. Even if we change our own views and resulting behaviors, we must still contend with the broader society's entrenched views of power and control over children. Developing a critical understanding of how power and control operate at individual, group, institutional, and systemic levels allows us to live within current systems more intentionally and with greater awareness.[5]

Liberation allows us the chance to critically choose values, thoughts, and patterns of response, rather than mindlessly perpetuating those that have become automatic through our socialization. We regain the ability to choose from a range of responses grounded in our awareness, critical thinking, intuition, and decision-making.[6] I aspire to be with the children in my life with this kind of awareness and intentionality so that I can live free from unexamined values, thoughts, and behaviors learned through a socialization process that continues the systems of oppression and perpetuates power over and control of others.[7]

Liberation parenting is praxis—action and critical reflection—applied to parent-child relationships. It requires us to leave behind our dominant socialization and to instead develop authentic and respectful relationships with the children in our lives.[8]

By moving into a liberatory consciousness in my parenting, what I hope is to ensure that Martel and Greyson believe that the full range of choices about who they are and how they want to be in the world are possible. Indeed, I wish that for all children. From choices as simple as hair length and color of clothing, to feeling and experiencing the full range of human emotions, to more complex choices such as life/love partners, I hope that Greyson and Martel experience the freedom to express their authentic selves while supporting those around them to do the same.

We often think of the words freedom and liberation in terms of big actions and social movements. Our goal as parents committed to liberation from power and control is to see freedom and liberation in our everyday actions and interactions. From those everyday actions, however, greater social change may one day grow.

CHAPTER FIVE

Tools for Transformation and Change

IN ORDER TO make real our commitment to freedom and liberation, we must engage in a transformation that requires a variety of processes, skills, knowledge, and tools. When we change our everyday behaviors to reflect and reinforce the internal change process, we begin to also change how, where, and when we focus our energy and time. Whereas before we may have been focused on the behaviors of children that didn't fit into our socialized notions of how they should behave, we can shift our frame of reference so that we offer children an opportunity to explore the world around them, make meaning of their experiences in the world, and create a deeper understanding of who they are and what they want from this life.

In this chapter, I'll share information about transformative learning and why it is critical to the change we need to embrace as parents. I'll also share various processes, strategies, and tools for transformative learning and address some common obstacles.

You may be looking for ways to address very specific challenges in your relationship with the children in your life. I'll share examples of how these tools, strategies, and processes can change the dynamics of controlling parenting, as well as provide opportunities for further reflection and change.

I won't tell you how to handle a fight between siblings, or how to help a child negotiate a difficult relationship with a friend. My most important message to you is that if you're facing challenges in your relationship with a child, if you're feeling discomfort that might be manifesting as fear, anger, or frustration, you have an opportunity to go inward and deal with whatever may be left from your past experiences that prevents you from being open, clear, and present with the child in your life.

Transformative Learning

The work we have to do is not about the children in our lives. It's about us, the parents. We need to engage in a transformative learning process that challenges our assumption that childhood is a long socialization process for adults-in-training who would not be able to develop without adults being in control and using power over them. I use the term *transformative learning* because I'm asking us to engage in a process that opens up our current worldview and transforms our understandings of childhood and adulthood.

As we grow up, we make meaning of the world through our experiences. When something happens to us, we expect the same thing to happen again in the future. We develop a frame of reference based on these experiences, and we adopt values, beliefs, and behaviors through living our daily lives. Most often, we absorb them without any critical examination.[1]

In order to transform this frame of reference, we must begin to differentiate ourselves from the institutions, groups, family units, and organizations that helped to form it. This process of moving away from the collective—those groups who helped form our worldview—is called individuation.[2]

Individuation is a critical component of the transformative learning process. To open up and transform our frame of reference or worldview, we must critically examine the beliefs, values, and behaviors that we have absorbed unconsciously.[3] Individuation leads to authenticity, another important component of transformative learning. Through individuation, we develop an understanding of who we are and what we believe; authenticity is the process of acting on that understanding. Ultimately, individuation and authenticity transform our understanding of the world and help us learn new ways of being and behaving.

The ability to be authentic in our relationships is a direct reflection of our understanding of ourselves. We cannot be authentic if we don't know who we are. We need to develop a conscious relationship to ourselves in order to be authentic. We can begin to look for ways to conduct our relationships with others and participate in our communities in an authentic way. The more authentic we become, the more we express that authentic self, the more we are transformed.[4]

We must take responsibility for our own development and individuation in order to be in authentic relationships with the children in our lives.[5] We must engage in a process of identifying and caring for our own needs so that our relationships with children are not burdened by them. Knowing ourselves and transforming our inner lives can create a way of approaching our children and our relationships without our vision clouded by our past hurtful experiences as children.

Let's be clear: our work as parents isn't about doing things differently so our children will change. It's not about finding the magic words or methods that will ensure compliance and eliminate all disagreements. Instead, it's about examining ourselves so that we can see how our ways of being with children have been constrained by our previously held beliefs, values, and attitudes. We do this so that we can experience authentic relationships with the children we love and so that they can live their own lives, free of our baggage.

Each of us will have different triggers. You may not have the same issues with food that I do, but perhaps you feel challenged by the issue of media control in a way that I do not. Whatever the issue, the change begins within each of us.

We cannot change the fact that adults have inherent power that children do not have, whether from physical size and maturity or from cultural processes. I am asking us to engage in a transformational process as parents, however, because through significant internal transformation we can work to ensure that the power dynamics between adults and children are not controlling and harmful to children. Our internal transformation leads to transformation of our relationships.

The process of transformative learning is not linear. It is a spiral process in which we revisit issues from different angles and perspectives. We enter in and out of the process; we experience critical incidents and integrate them; we move back and forth. We may wish for a more direct approach to change, having been socialized to understand learning as a linear process with a fixed goal. True transformation, however, comes through traveling a spiral path.

Mistakes and Guilt

As the transformative learning process begins, we often reflect on our past behaviors of controlling and diminishing children. As we progress, we can't always live up to the ideals we have about how to live with children respectfully and lovingly. We experience cognitive dissonance when our thoughts or actions are out of line with our ideals, and feelings of guilt, shame, and anger are normal reactions.

During the first few years that I tried to live according to my values of justice, freedom, and liberation with Martel and Greyson, I carried a lot of guilt and shame for my past and ongoing mistakes. These feelings still come up for me today.

Thankfully, I've also come to see my journey as a parent from a longer view. I remind myself that I spent over four decades immersed in a paradigm of control and domination. During that time, I was unaware of the impact it had on me as a child and an adult. Unlearning my socialization and conditioning is a slow process where I move up and down the spiral of transformative learning. As I have worked to unlearn ideas about children, I have also unlearned some of my socialization about mistakes.

As children, we learn in school and often from parents that mistakes are bad and lead to punishment or humiliation. I know that as a child I strongly associated mistakes at school and at home with punishment, humiliation, and shame. Even in college and law school, I continued to feel humiliation when I made mistakes while learning. Yet mistakes are as natural and inevitable as successes, and need not engender shame. Indeed, mistakes can be a valuable part of the learning process, helping us better understand what we *do* want by showing us what we *don't* want.

We may fear that accepting our mistakes means that we will have no motivation to change our future behavior. We have accepted the need for conditional approval and believe that we must punish ourselves with feelings of guilt and shame to ensure that we will not repeat the mistake. Contrary to our assumption, acceptance of mistakes is absolutely compatible with a desire to grow and improve—in fact, it is an essential tool for growth. Without the learning that comes from examining our mistakes from a neutral perspective, we are hampered in our desire to learn a new way of being.

I haven't completely shed the performance expectations that I internalized throughout my life. I'm able to see the mistakes of children as part of the learning process, and slowly I'm applying that principle of learning to myself. I see now that fear of making a mistake and experiencing potential shame and humiliation only serves the broader paradigm of control and keeps us from reaching out to others in our learning process.

Guilt also serves to immobilize us and keep us from further examining our behavior. When I feel guilty about something I've done, I'm much less willing to examine my behavior from a distance. I want to avoid the feelings of guilt, so I avoid any consideration of my behavior. I also look to others to absolve me of my guilt—often those who've been hurt by my actions, like Martel and Greyson.

To counteract guilt, I remind myself that I am both a product of my socialization and a learner on the path of a new way of being. I reflect on the need to examine my behaviors from a neutral standpoint in order to learn from them and progress up the learning spiral.

In addressing guilt and mistakes, I hope to encourage us to feel what we feel and allow those feelings to move through us. Accepting our feelings is another important step towards transformative learning.

Accepting Our Feelings

Accepting the inevitability of our mistakes opens us further to the transformative learning process. Similarly, acceptance of our feelings, in all their forms, allows us to move through them and move on without damaging ourselves or our relationships.

As children, we may have experienced the judgment of our parents and other authority figures of the emotions they perceived as negative. We internalize this experience of conditional acceptance of feelings. Good feelings, we learn, can be shared; bad feelings must be hidden.

If we allow our feelings to run their course, we have the opportunity to integrate those experiences into a pattern of healthy functioning. If we judge our feelings and resist them, they don't go away, but take on a life of their own. They become part of the way we function at an unconscious level. One step in our transformative process is to bring to consciousness the very fact that we have been unconscious.

As a child, I felt required to hide many of my emotions that were viewed as negative by my parents, such as anger, sadness, or frustration. I have difficulty accepting these emotions in myself today because I deeply internalized the messages I received as a child. I regulated my emotions based on what I learned was acceptable to others. As a result, I've spent much of my adult life trying to reign in my emotions. As a child and an adult, I had a lot of anger, which I now realize was partly due to how much I was controlled and forced to behave by adults in order to receive the acceptance and love I needed. I felt my anger was all-consuming and I worked for many years to push the anger below the surface and keep it at bay for fear that I would hurt myself or those I loved.

As I began the process of re-forming a life that had more integrity and authenticity, I struggled mightily with allowing myself to feel the full range of emotions that I'd suppressed for so many years. In many ways, trying to unconditionally accept the emotions of Martel and Greyson has been freeing for me as well.

But with the freedom has come a lot of fear: fear of unleashing my anger and frustration from a life lived according to others' rules. Fear that my anger would hurt those around me. Fear that they would find me unlovable. Unconditional acceptance and love for Martel and Greyson means little if I can't apply it to myself.

As I uncover my feelings and fears one by one, I'm slowly learning to accept them as part of who I am. I'm challenging and exposing the socialization and conditioning that led me to believe that it wasn't legitimate to feel the way I felt. As a result, I'm able to reduce the ways I am triggered by the children in my life and approach them more authentically and lovingly.

It's a paradox: I need to embrace my anger and fear in order to lessen their hold on me. Accepting who I am, fully, is part of the process of deconstructing the paradigm of control that I accepted as a child and perpetuated as an adult.

At times, this acceptance process seems painfully slow. I want to be able to say, "Yes! It is okay for me to feel angry or hurt or upset. My feelings are legitimate." And yet resistance arises. It goes back and forth: acceptance – control – acceptance – control. In resisting these feelings, I have found they grow much more powerful. This reinforces my fear and my instinct to impose control until I am able to consciously take a step away from the vicious cycle.

Reflecting on a day I spent with Greyson reinforces for me the power of this resistance. On this particular day, Greyson and I planned to run many errands. Part of our plan was to go to the toy store, at Greyson's request, before grocery shopping. Between the first and second stops, Greyson, who was three at the time, told me that he wanted to go to Wal-Mart. I had a negative internal reaction, but suppressed it and said, "Okay, we'll go to Wal-Mart." Five minutes later, I pulled into the parking lot and he said, in a disappointed voice, "Why are we at Wal-Mart?".

I reacted with anger, saying to him, "The only reason we're at Wal-Mart is because you asked to come." I am sure I said this at least three times with increasing intensity. "I didn't want to come to Wal-Mart; you did." I asked him if he wanted to go in, and he said no, he wanted to go to the toy store.

I kept going in my vicious cycle and lectured him about the fact that once we left Wal-Mart we would not be coming back. I was thinking, I drove a mile out of my way—yes, *one whole mile!*—to come to the store and now he doesn't want to go in!

It was very quiet in the back seat when we left Wal-Mart. Once I was back on the road, I came back to center a bit and apologized to Greyson. He didn't respond. Of course, I really wanted him to say, "It's okay, Mom!". I wanted a three year old child to absolve me of my guilt about yelling. I wanted *him* to take care of *my* needs.

I adjusted the rear view mirror and saw a defeated, sad little boy staring out the window. Of course, while I was in angry lecture mode I was not looking at him and chose not to see how my words, tone, and volume were hurting him. When I looked at him, I could clearly see that he was in pain.

It was a low moment for me to see how I had wounded this person whom I love so much. He was so little and vulnerable, and yet his feelings were as big as mine. I had used my power as an adult to dominate, shame, and hurt him. Despite this, he still loved me, but I knew I had created distrust, fear, and resentment.

Fear of my own anger resurfaced. I felt guilty and disgusted with myself. I so wanted to push down the anger inside of me.

When Greyson first asked me to go to Wal-Mart, I was annoyed and angry. I'd already agreed to take him to the toy store. Why should I have to go to another store? Instead of acknowledging, even just to myself, that I was angry that he would even ask, I pushed away my feelings. I resisted my anger and tried to talk myself into feeling better rather than allowing and accepting how I felt.

I decided to perform, to pretend to be something I was not at that moment. Instead of disappearing, my anger grew to the point that Greyson's change of mind (quite typical of a three year old) triggered an explosion of all my pent-up feelings.

This was, of course, not the first time I resisted my feelings only to explode at a later time. Despite my desire to create a parenting paradigm that is based on respect, not domination, I fall short of my ideals. My childhood was spent waiting to become an adult so that I would matter as much as the adults around me did. When I feel as though my needs don't matter to others, I am triggered and I get angry.

But by denying my feelings of anger, I disregard myself. I perpetuate the disempowerment I experienced in my childhood. Instead of owning up to my role and my power in this cycle, I choose to focus my anger on the person who is less powerful than me, in this case Greyson. I fall into "parent as a victim of the child" mode. Ironically, when I accept all the parts of myself, I come much closer to liberating myself from this dominant paradigm.

As a parent, if you find yourself resisting your anger or frustration, you might ask yourself "why?". Is it possible to learn to be angry in a way that isn't destructive? Often, the way anger was expressed in my home as a child was hurtful and manipulative. Therefore, I suppressed my own anger as an adult because I didn't want to hurt those around me. Identifying the beginnings of those feelings of anger and expressing them before they become explosive and hurtful is a strategy that I'm trying to use more and more in my learning process.

The reality is that as humans, we will feel anger, frustration, sadness, and disappointment. Life will not always be on an upswing. Often, when I'm in the midst of pushing away my feelings, Rob will say, "Lean into the punch," a loving reminder to me that if I give myself permission to feel whatever I feel, I can move through the feelings more quickly and authentically.

If our goal as parents is to create space for children to be who they are, we also need to create that space for ourselves. However, acknowledgement and acceptance of our feelings doesn't mean we absolve ourselves of responsibility for actions that are hurtful to others. The purpose of accepting our feelings is to allow ourselves to feel them fully, to consider and reflect upon why we were triggered, and to integrate that experience so that we move up the learning spiral. If we're in a place where our feelings may be truly harmful, we may need to walk away to feel the full force of them and come back when our expression will be less intense for those around us.

As I've said in other sections, the discomfort that comes from the challenges in our relationship with children is an opportunity to turn inward. I may have been angry at Greyson for asking to go to

Wal-Mart and then changing his mind—but my anger was my issue, not his. I don't need him to change his desires, thoughts, or behavior to take care of my anger. I want him to be able to ask for what he wants and also to change his mind. What I need to do is learn from my own feelings why I reacted with such anger and create a different way of responding when I feel the kind of anger that allowed me to diminish his humanity.

Mindfulness

As we have discussed, fear is often the core of mainstream cultural beliefs about childhood and children's behaviors. We're often overtaken by fear of the future, of what will happen if we don't socialize our children to fit into the collective norms of society. When, as parents, we let this fear cloud our relationship with children, we are motivated to control and dehumanize them.

"Autopilot parenting" is another major challenge. We are creatures of habit, and often create patterns of behavior that we replay over and over in similar situations. When our child acts in a certain way, we react in the same ways we have reacted before, without considering different possibilities. One of the ways we can overcome fear and automatic reactions, and also redefine our relationships with children, is mindfulness.

We often connect mindfulness to meditation. I'll be honest and say that I've tried meditation and not found it particularly helpful. Perhaps I'm not a very good meditator. I know other parents who do find it helpful and are able to meditate on a regular basis.

Even if you don't meditate, mindfulness can still be an important process in creating connected, supportive parent/child relationships. Don't skip to the next section if you don't meditate!

There are different ways of achieving mindfulness or being present in the moment.

I have found simply focusing on the here and now to be extremely helpful. Focusing on the present moment, rather than allowing my mind to race forward into the future or backwards into some hurtful past, helps me avoid the traps of fear and habit and instead respond authentically to the situation.

In studying mindfulness, researchers have found that mindfulness not only had positive impacts on mothers, but also resulted in behavioral changes in their children—even though the mindfulness training was focused solely on mothers.[6] In one study, mothers of children with autism were directed not to try to change their children's behavior, but to be mindful and present. Positive behavioral changes occurred in children, because the mothers were able to move away from imposing their will on their children and controlling them in order to alter their behavior. The mothers in the study reported feeling less frustration and anger as a result of their mindfulness practice.[7]

Mindfulness can begin with the realization of the need for unconditional acceptance of another person and oneself, including nonjudgmental acceptance of behaviors.[8] *Nonjudgmental acceptance* may sound like ignoring problematic behaviors, but that isn't what it means. The difference is that behavior is responded to without any accompanying judgment, such as "I'm a bad person," "I'm disappointed in her," or "This always happens; you'll never learn." By approaching behaviors without judgment, we can see that parents and children have needs that may be different and sometimes in conflict, but are connected and interdependent.

Another way of thinking about mindfulness is the idea of emptying our minds of everything except what is happening right in that moment. By moving aside the clutter of fear, anger, or limiting beliefs about the situation we face, we can often use our intuition to guide us in finding new possibilities that we may not have been able to even consider before.

One nuanced way of being mindful is to not try to analyze why something is happening, but to just be there and present during the event. I remember a time when Greyson was three and we were at a store. He wanted desperately to buy a toy that we couldn't afford at that moment. We went back and forth: I tried to explain why we couldn't buy it, he told me that he wanted to buy it.

Finally, I stopped trying to fix his feelings. I stopped worrying about other people around me. We sat down together on the floor in a place where there were fewer people. I just held him. I stopped thinking about why he should or shouldn't feel the way he felt. I stopped thinking about how I could convince him to feel differently. In fact, it seemed as though time just stopped. He put his head on my lap and I stroked his hair. We were at peace together. In a few minutes he was ready to get up.

Mindful parenting is not always easy for me. I am often too preoccupied with my own thoughts and feelings to be present in the moment. For example, when I'm in the middle of some task or my mind is racing about what needs to be done that day, I'm much more reactionary if a conflict comes up between Martel and Greyson. I go into "break up the fight" mode, without really seeing what is happening between them. However, the positive results I get for myself when I remember to be mindful are a great reinforcement for me to continue to work on my mindfulness and presence.

Sometimes I use a word or phrase to get me into the place where I'm not reacting. For example, when Martel and Greyson are yelling at each other (playfully or not), I'll often say to myself, "This is *my* issue, not theirs." I know that discord between Martel and Greyson is a trigger for me because I haven't cleared all of my emotional issues around sibling harmony (or disharmony). My self-reminder helps me pay attention to what is really happening and stay focused in the moment. This acknowledgment and awareness that so many of my challenges are my own issues isn't a denial of my feelings. Rather, it serves to acknowledge my feelings in a meaningful way that moves me out of reaction.

For some, it may not be a phrase that's helpful to bring us back to the here and now, but it might be a pebble or token in our pocket, or perhaps a bracelet or piece of jewelry that serves as a touchstone—anything that helps us get ourselves out of an automatic reaction and back to what is happening in front of us.

Awareness

I use the term *awareness* differently from *mindfulness*. While *mindfulness* means remaining connected to the present moment, *awareness* means observing how our beliefs and behaviors impact those around us.

Accepting feedback about our behavior from others, without excuses or defensiveness, is one way to develop awareness. With younger children, we may get immediate feedback about behaviors that are disempowering and hurtful when the child yells or cries. As children get older, they may be able to give us verbal feedback about our behaviors and the impact on their lives.

Another step toward developing awareness is to take time to reflect on our experiences as children and as parents. Our goal in this reflection is to understand how our own childhood experiences have influenced our current view of childhood, children, and the role of parents/adults.

When we're faced with conflict and challenge in our relationship with children, this can be an opportunity to pause and create further awareness of how we may be using power and control. When we're experiencing emotional turmoil, this may be another call to pause and create an expanded awareness. Of all the aspects of the process of liberation, I believe self-awareness is the absolute foundation. Understanding who we are, how we relate to the world, how we view others, and the issues of power and control is critical to creating change in ourselves and ultimately broader social change for all children.

When I work with parents to develop more awareness of adult power and control, I ask them to reflect on two things. First, I ask them to think about a specific instance when they felt disempowered as a child and to identify the feelings that were associated with that incident. Next, I ask them to think about a time when they felt empowered as a child and to identify the feelings associated with that. In examining those experiences, my goal is to interrogate our childhoods from a perspective of power dynamics. Often, our own experiences of disempowerment can serve as triggers in our relationships with children.

When I've asked these questions of parents, they can often come up with many instances of feeling powerless, but have more trouble thinking of times when they felt empowered. More often, when discussing feeling empowered, I have heard experiences of individuals who as adults were finally able to challenge a controlling or dominating parent. Rarely have I heard a story of a child who felt empowered.

Another common experience is the struggle to name the feelings associated with experiences of disempowerment. We may bury these feelings as they're painful to expose. We may have fear about opening old wounds and dealing with what comes out. We may also have learned as children that our feelings were of little importance in the adult world, leading us to push our anger and frustration down in order to get along with those who were more powerful and controlling.

Each of us had both unique experiences and universal experiences as children. In working with and talking to parents, I find that we have many common experiences of feeling powerless. We may also feel as though our needs as children weren't met, for whatever reason. It may be that our parents did their best, but because of economic pressure, they were stressed and had limited time with us in between working and struggling to make ends meet. It may be that we came from a single-parent household and felt we had to take on responsibilities before we were ready in order to help our parent. It may be that we came from a home that was very authoritarian and controlling. I've only known a small handful of adults who grew up in such a way that they felt they were accepted for who they were and had the freedom to explore and grow in ways that were meaningful for them.

Creating greater awareness of the dynamics of power and control facilitates the process of moving through our feelings of disempowerment. We can understand the commonality of this experience and become more self-aware, able to see how we operate from such a system and to challenge our automatic assumptions and reactions.

Identifying Our Triggers

Many of us believe that we've overcome the past and moved beyond our painful childhood experiences—until we have children and the feelings resurface. Because our interactions with children are intricately linked with our own childhood experiences, we can easily be triggered by the actions of children. I know that I'm triggered when, in a split second, something Martel or Greyson does has me full of rage, anger, or sadness far out of proportion to the specific incident. Paying attention to the moments when we're triggered as parents can be the opening to examining our experiences of powerlessness.

One parent I spoke with found herself triggered when her son would want to eat all of a particular food that was in the house without considering that others might want to eat it as well. When she commented to him that this was not fair to others, he would respond that they could go buy more, which felt unreasonable and demanding to her.

She knew that her response was out of proportion to what the child was asking, yet, of course, she felt it just the same. After some questioning and self-reflection, she realized that as a child she had been considered selfish for asking for anything. This disempowering experience stayed with her, shaping her view of appropriate childhood behavior and resurfacing in response to her son's desires. Once she made the connection between her emotional response to her son and her own experience as a child of being made to feel selfish and ungrateful, she could more easily accept where she was and move forward from it.

When our feelings and triggers remain unexamined, we often end up in a loop of action and reaction. Rather than acting and then reflecting on our actions, we stay in reaction mode. Being in reaction can move us to want to use control and force, as opposed to looking for ways to meet everyone's needs.

Exploring the uniqueness of our experiences while acknowledging some of the more universal experiences can be an empowering process for parents to move beyond the place of reaction. What is a trigger for one parent may not be for another, and sometimes it is easier to identify another person's disproportionate reactions than our own. Because of this, we can help each other to identify possible triggers. Coming together with other parents to discuss these experiences can also give us a sense of solidarity as we work through the issues. Though some may think of this as therapy, I see it as a process of understanding who we are and how our experiences impact our current worldview and block our ability to move into more authentic relationships with children.

For example, if I could have disabled my triggered reaction to Greyson changing his mind about going to Wal-Mart, I might have merely said, "We came because you asked to. Do you still want to go in?". If he said no, I could've just turned around and gone on to our next destination. No anger, no shame.

What I wasn't able to discern in the moment, because I'd pushed down my anger, was that as a child I was afraid to ask for what I wanted. Sometimes this was because my parents were struggling financially, other times it was because I perceived that expressing my desires would cause further pressure on a dysfunctional family dynamic. My desire was to remain as unnoticed as possible so as to avoid negative attention being directed at me.

Greyson has no such inhibitions. He openly asks for what he wants and sometimes we're able to give it to him and other times we're not. He is still free, despite some of my reactions to his expressed wants.

Knowing our triggers allows us to better anticipate when we might be triggered by a situation. It also helps us understand and identify the feelings associated with being triggered, so that we can disable those triggers early on in situations with children rather than allow them to lead us into reactionary behavior.

Knowledge

Reading about the thoughts, experiences, and challenges of other parents who are working toward developing a relationship with children based on respect and trust can help us to continue to challenge the paradigm within which we were socialized. If I cannot find examples of this respect and trust in my own experiences, reading about how others do this expands my view of the world. The internet has a wealth of resources, including blogs, online discussion groups, articles, and websites. Books focused on respectful parenting can also add to our understanding of what this can look like in our lives.[9]

Growing up in a paradigm of domination and control, we internalized much information about children that is in fact *mis*information. If, for example, our parents required us to sit quietly at the dinner table at the age of two, and we were scolded for not doing so, we may have internalized the belief that it's developmentally appropriate to expect a two year old to be able to sit through dinner without making noise or disrupting adult conversation. If we were punished for wetting the bed at age five, we may believe that all five year olds should be able to get through the night without an accident.

Examining what we *think* we know about children is perhaps the most important knowledge we can acquire. Once we've developed awareness about our biases and assumptions about how children should behave or what they should be doing, we can begin to study the children in our lives to find out who they are without the filter of our socialization. Generalizations about childhood and child development can be valuable, but we need to cultivate a thirst for knowledge about the children closest to us.

By identifying and setting aside our biases, we can observe from a more neutral standpoint what's happening in children's lives and how they respond to particular things. We can talk with them about what's in their hearts and on their minds and listen without judgment in order to gain greater knowledge about who they really are. If we accept them without judgment, we have the opportunity to know them in ways we cannot if our love and approval are conditional on them behaving in ways that please us but are not authentic for them.

Even if we think we know them, we can suspend this "knowing" and allow children to reveal themselves to us in the timeframe and manner that best suits them. Often when Martel is upset, I want to interrogate him so that I can help him deal with what is bothering him. But there are times when he doesn't want me to talk to him, and I need to respect those times as much as I appreciate the times when he is willing to share his deepest feelings with me.

Often our children are most vulnerable and open during quiet times, such as when they're going to sleep or when it's just the two of you together with no expectations of doing something. Being open in those quiet moments—not forcing them, but allowing them to be—can deepen trust and build a connected and respectful relationship between child and parent.

If we're committed to liberation from domination and control, we need to step back from seeing the parent-child relationship as top-down, with the adult handing down knowledge and information to the child. What adults often call *sharing our wisdom* is really a way of couching our need to have children accept our point-of-view as correct. Instead, we need to approach the relationship as a mutual opportunity to gain knowledge about a perspective different from our own.

We can open ourselves up to learning about children just as we might open ourselves to learning a new culture and language. If we approach this new culture and language from a desire to know and understand it, as opposed to a desire to mold and change it, we can engage in co-creation. Our worldview combined with the worldview of children can come together. We recreate our understanding and, together, change our world.

When I think about interacting with children as if I were a visitor in a new culture, I remember a time when I was uncomfortable with a particular way of being among Martel and his friends when they play video games. They sometimes became very intense and spoke to each other in ways that sounded harsh to me. When Martel would get intense, I worried that he was hurting his friends' feelings and they wouldn't want to play video games with him. I imposed my expectations and worldview on to what was happening between them and I would often intervene.

These interventions started to get frustrating for Martel and I could also see that he was beginning to feel bad about himself. After reflecting on my actions and assumptions, I realized that I did not know whether Martel was hurting his friends' feelings. So I began to ask questions to test my assumption. I might say, "How's everyone doing?", or "Is everyone having fun doing this?". More often than not, everyone was fine. It was my view, my "knowledge," that was skewed.

In addition to being open to my own need to continue learning and acquiring new knowledge, I of course have a role in facilitating Martel and Greyson's learning process. Just as I share information with them about how to add numbers or spell a word, I share information with them about social norms such as expectations that may be in place when we go places or visit people.

For example, one set of grandparents established a rule about only eating in the kitchen. When we visit, if Martel or Greyson forgets and starts to take food into the living room, I remind him. Similarly, if we are visiting a museum, theme park, city pool, or restaurant, I might remind them of the rules and expectations we will need to respect while we are there.

Some may believe that liberation and freedom result in anarchy. In fact, sharing information is an important part of my parenting process and also deepens the trust between us, resulting in cooperation. I explain the reasons why, when I need to say "no" or ask Martel or Greyson to change his behavior. This gives them the opportunity to make an authentic choice to align with me, whereas if I attempted to coerce their behavior or denied them information with a statement like "because I said so" or "because I am the mommy" I would rob them of the chance to make that authentic choice.

I need to continue to be aware of the power dynamics that may always exist between the children who share my life and myself as the adult. Although we may be engaged in a co-creation process, if I have a particular outcome in mind and I'm not forthright with myself or them, then I'm not engaging in a process that is respectful or that increases trust and understanding between us. Continuing to engage in a learning process that expands and deepens my knowledge of how power operates and may manifest in my own relationships allows me to continue on the path of respectful parenting.

Perspective Taking

In any relationship, the ability to see the other person's perspective can build trust and reinforce the connection between two individuals. In relationships where there are power differentials, perspective taking by the individual who benefits from more institutional power is critical to breaking down the differential and working toward equal relationships. In looking at the impact of perspective taking, researchers have found that it induces empathy. When we have empathy toward an individual we improve our attitudes toward the person and toward the social group with which they are identified (for example, on the basis of race, gender, sexual orientation, or age). Perspective taking thus takes on an important role in reducing bias, prejudice, and discrimination.[10]

In our socialization process, our views of children are shaped by how we view them as a group. Perspective taking allows us to move beyond our own view of the world to see another individual's (or group's) perspective and thus gain empathy for their experiences, particularly when we might be in conflict.

After arriving home after a long day out with Greyson, I was ready for a break and dinner and he wanted to play. We were discussing a set of penguins that belonged to Martel, who was gone at the time, and I was reluctant to give them to Greyson without knowing whether Martel would agree.

Greyson can be quite persistent when he wants something. This is a good trait to have in life, but for a tired parent who just wants compliance, it's a setup for disempowerment. Instead of listening to Greyson, I became frustrated and impatient. I interrupted him and told him that the penguins were Martel's and we could not play with them until Martel got home. He started to say something else and in my frustration I tossed the box on the floor and said, "Fine, just do whatever you want with them." I walked out of the room.

Greyson walked out of the bedroom a few seconds later and said, "Mom, ask Martel when he gets home if I can play with the penguins." This is probably what he had planned to say all along, but I kept interrupting him because I felt as though he was not listening to me. My desire was for him to comply without argument. When he started to engage in more conversation, I assumed he was going to make a case for playing with the penguins before Martel came home.

In some ways, the whole scenario seems quite petty. I was angry about eight little plastic penguins! But as I reflected on my behavior and emotions during the exchange the next day, I thought about how much I had wanted Greyson to understand me and how much that desire had colored the whole interaction. I believed that if he had understood my perspective, he would have seen what I needed him to do and he would have done it. What struck me was how *I* had resisted seeing and understanding *Greyson's* perspective.

In my relationship with Greyson, I have the power. When under stress, I've used my power to force him to accept or at least give in to my point of view, while at the same time I claim feelings of powerlessness. I talk over him, interrupt him, and coerce him. I close myself off and refuse to see his perspective. In all of this, I dehumanize him—and myself.

Finally, after pushing myself to admit that I had wanted Greyson to see my perspective but I had refused to see his, I broke down and let go of all my resistance. I remember openly claiming to Rob that I was stuck in my own worldview, and I let myself accept my choice to not take in Greyson's perspective. I owned it. As always happens, my resistance to accepting the "negative" parts of myself had caused my feelings of frustration to increase.

As discussed before, accepting my choice to disregard Greyson's perspective did not mean that I intended to continue doing so. It was not an abandonment of my goal of living a life that affirmed Greyson's rights to respect and dignity. Instead, I accepted the place I had been in at that moment and shed the guilt and shame that interfered with my ability to reflect neutrally on the experience, learn from it, and move forward.

In some ways, it's easy to articulate what Greyson's perspective might have been. At three, he was struggling with manipulating the physical world to meet his needs. He has always had a strong desire to do things himself and was still developing his ability to use his hands and tools to create his desired outcomes. The world, at that age, was still out of his reach. He needed our help to get things down, or to lift him up. He sometimes asked for help negotiating sharing toys with other children. And he resisted our attempts to help him when he did not want help.

Intellectually, I could "see" his perspective. But I was choosing not to feel his perspective deep within me. This surface-level acceptance allowed me to ignore the warning of my feelings of frustration and to feel justified in continuing to dominate him and push my own agenda. A deeper acceptance, first of my "negative" impulses and feelings, and then subsequently of his perspective, would have created an opening where I could respond with compassion and love both to Greyson and to myself. Rather than needing to reinforce my own position in order to solidify my power, I could have chosen to see how my actions can create powerlessness. Accepting our past, our mistakes, and all of our feelings as valuable parts of ourselves is a process of reintegration. Although we're accountable for our actions, we can move beyond blame for playing the roles assigned to us in the system of oppression.[11] Blame, like guilt, serves the system of oppression by keeping us in the ditch looking for who is at fault for pushing us there.

Often when I'm in a place of frustration and beginning to focus my anger outwardly at Martel or Greyson, a word or two from Rob or another parent can help bring me back. I have heard the offer "Is there anything I can do to help?" as a call for me to pause and give in to whatever I am feeling at the moment. It can help me create awareness about myself and the situation so that I can move forward with more intentionality.

Other Strategies and Skills

Developing a set of tools with which to change our attitudes, beliefs, and behaviors is a must in transforming our role as parents. Some of the tools I've used to transform my thinking about the nature of adult power and control are tools that I used in my professional life and now apply to my personal life. I also acquired new tools as a parent. Some of the tools were very helpful in the beginning as I wanted to move quickly in my unlearning process. Others did not become useful until later. The use of tools ebbs and flows depending on what my needs and challenges are.

Writing and reflecting on my struggles as a parent and putting them in the context of a broader paradigm of domination and control are, for me, critical parts of my growth. In this way, I use tools from other relationships—work, teaching, facilitation—and adapt them to parenting. You might examine the current set of tools you use in other areas of your life to see whether or not they can help you in your process.

Often we may find ourselves in an avalanche of emotions, as I described in my experience with Greyson in the car. Stopping ourselves in the midst of this destructive reactionary mode isn't easy. When I am not able to physically step away and take some time out, I've learned (sometimes!) to stop myself before my words or actions become hurtful.

One strategy I've found effective is to look Martel or Greyson in the eyes when I feel like I'm losing it. During the incident with Greyson in the car, I didn't stop the car to turn around and look at him. In that moment, I wasn't seeing him as a person, as a human being. He was a trigger; he was annoying; he was anything but a smaller human being who had a strong desire to go to the store but needed me to help make that happen because he was too small to do it himself.

If I had looked him in the eyes, I would've seen the person, the human with a heart and soul, the child I love. Instead I allowed myself to act out by not looking at him. One of the strategies for training soldiers going into war is to dehumanize the enemy. This detachment strategy allows soldiers to carry out their objective of killing others more easily, because they're not seen as human.[12] Although this comparison might seem extreme, when I'm not looking at Martel and Greyson and seeing their faces, their eyes, their reactions, their hearts, it's much easier to hurt them when I'm angry. I momentarily dehumanize them and rationalize my own behavior as acceptable.

In fact, it is generally when I'm detached from Martel and Greyson that I find myself dehumanizing them. This detachment can be emotional, intellectual, or physical. If I'm in another room trying to get something done, Greyson calling for me can be a huge trigger. I can't even count the number of times Greyson has called out my name when I'm in the midst of something and after my irritated response called back happily, "I love you, Mom!". If I'm in the midst of some thought while driving with him and I'm not focused on what he's saying, I can easily find myself feeling frustrated and taking my frustration out on him.

This in no way means that I believe I should be next to him at all times or only be waiting for the next time he starts a conversation with me. But it does mean that I need to be more vigilant about how I react to him when I'm disengaged and have a desire to stay in my own thoughts or activity. I may still feel frustrated by the interruption, but by reconnecting quickly with him—coming close, looking him in the eyes, or quickly glancing back at him in the rearview mirror—I'm less likely to act on this frustration with anger. I can mindfully acknowledge the frustration, or the fact that I was thinking about something else, or the need to complete a task, without lashing out at him because I'm not connected to him.

Sometimes it is helpful for me to discuss my needs openly with Martel and Greyson—not to make them responsible for meeting my needs, but as part of how I take responsibility for them myself. When I need to buy myself some time or need to process how I'm feeling about something, I may say, "I need a minute to think about this and make a decision," or "I'm starting to feel frustrated and need to take a break for a few minutes." I've even said, "If I do this right now I think I'm going to get frustrated or angry and I don't want to yell. Let's ask your dad (or let me take a time out)."

If I'm already in reactionary mode and starting to yell, sometimes I'm able to just close my mouth. Physically putting my hand over my mouth sometimes helps as well. If the situation at hand doesn't require my immediate physical presence, I may just walk out of the room and give myself a time out.

I've also used techniques such as EFT (Emotional Freedom Technique) to move through my emotions more quickly so that I can re-engage with Martel and Greyson.[13] I've used EFT with the help of practitioners to deal with deep emotions that I'm afraid to confront by myself. I've also used it to help me deal with a situation where my nerves are shot and I can't get out of a situation right away, like when I'm stuck in the car or on a plane.

Another tool I've used in examining my thoughts and attitudes is The Work, a technique developed by Byron Katie.[14] She espouses a step-by-step process to examine our thoughts. Ultimately she believes that it's not the situation but rather our thoughts about it that cause us anger or distress. If we're able to accept things as they are, in part by questioning the truth of our thoughts, we can transform our lives.

Often we have trouble, in Katie's terms, accepting *what is* with children. Greyson loves to play with toys. He had opened all his gifts on a particular occasion and by the end of the day was asking to open more presents. I went into "he never appreciates what he has" mode. This was my way of saying to myself that he didn't appreciate all of my work and generosity. Using The Work, I can interrogate the thought "he should appreciate me" by turning it around, saying, "I should appreciate him" or "I should appreciate myself" and considering whether those are just as true as the original thought. I often find that I don't give myself the respect and appreciation I deserve and want. I have the opportunity to examine whether or not it really is Greyson's role to make me feel appreciated or whether it is my responsibility to treat myself with respect and appreciation.

It can also be helpful to remind myself that their present reality is their reality. My wanting it to be different doesn't change their reality. When birthdays or holidays are built up to be big events, children are often disappointed when the end of the party or holiday comes. Why wouldn't Greyson feel disappointed that there weren't more gifts to open? His reality is what it is. Accepting his reality in that situation allowed me to give voice to his sadness that the big event was over.

It's also helpful to identify "red flag" words that accompany our assumptions. For example, being conscious of using the words *always* and *never* can help us identify that we're in a reactionary mode and move us to critical reflection. I've found myself saying about Greyson, "It doesn't matter what I do, he's *never* satisfied." If I apply that to the situation with the gifts and look at how Greyson reacted when he opened each gift, he showed genuine appreciation for each of his gifts with expressions of excitement and joy, followed by hugs. In that one "always" or "never" statement I had wiped away what really happened that day and replaced it with a different version of reality. Rarely are such absolute statements true.

In the beginning of my change process with Martel and Greyson, I would often post sticky notes with helpful words or phrases around the house to remind me to refocus on what was important to me. A mental focus word can also be useful: a word like *connection, respect, choice,* or whatever is meaningful to you at the time that you can call to mind to refocus and remind yourself of your goals.

A common technique I've read about on many respectful parenting forums and used myself is to reframe my behavior or beliefs, applying them to a parallel situation as an aid to examining their validity. By asking myself whether I would treat an adult or talk to a friend the way I talk to Martel or Greyson, I can shed light on my erroneous belief that it's acceptable to treat a child with less respect than an adult.

For example, I've seen many parents in play situations force a child to share her toys. To reframe this situation, I might ask myself how I would feel if Rob forced me to share my new car or favorite musical instrument with a visiting friend. If we wouldn't treat an adult or wouldn't want ourselves to be treated the way we are about to treat a child, it may be time to rethink why it's okay to treat a child with disrespect.

I've already mentioned in the section on mindfulness some techniques for being in the here and now. Other parents I know use yoga or meditation to center and find peace. I've also used the technique of counting to ten in my head or just breathing to re-center myself.

One parent I know used a timer as a tool during one of those periods where she was determined to improve her relationships but would go to bed every night disappointed because she had fallen back into the same old bad habits. She carried the timer, set for an hour or two hours depending on how things were going. Whenever it went off, she was reminded of her intentions and able to re-center herself. A watch with an hourly chime can be used the same way.

Sometimes I find I just need a change of scenery to dissipate a lot of negative energy. On a day trip to another city, I was in a huge reactionary mode to what was happening between Martel and Greyson in the back seat. I tried talking to myself, using EFT, reframing, and nothing was working. Finally, I pulled over at a McDonalds with a playscape because I knew I couldn't get myself redirected without getting out of the car for 15 or 20 minutes. Another time, while coordinating the kids getting into the car, I was so frustrated that I shut the car doors while they were strapped in, walked away, and yelled into the sky.

My goal in using any of these tools is not to deny my feelings or make them magically disappear. My feelings are real and need to be acknowledged, mostly by me. My goal is to find a release for my feelings that doesn't involve yelling at Martel or Greyson in ways that are hurtful, demeaning, and dehumanizing.

Asking for support for creating a liberation parenting model can be critical. We may find ourselves feeling isolated, as though we're alone in our battle to let go of control and domination as a parenting paradigm. This is especially true in the beginning of our process of letting go. I've met hundreds of parents in person and thousands online who are on this path and face the same struggles. Connecting with others can help normalize our struggles, give us strength for the challenging times, and move us forward.

Support and accountability go hand in hand in this process. We need to be able to admit our mistakes and open ourselves up beyond the façade we've created with others around us. However, if we surround ourselves with people who are willing to merely say, "It's okay, don't worry," without the additional challenge of questioning why we may be where we're at, we may find ourselves floundering and not moving forward in our process.

I've had the opportunity to create support online and in real life for my parenting process. Connecting with other parents who are struggling to let go of their socialization and create different relationships with their children allows me to discuss and share strategies, frustrations, and concerns. If you live in a small community, it may be difficult or impossible to find others near you who are on a similar path, but conferences, online communities, blogs, books, and YouTube videos can be ways to create community and enjoy feelings of solidarity and support. One of the reasons I began writing my website was to create accountability for myself. Admitting my mistakes, revealing the challenges through writing, and sharing this online have been part of making myself accountable for unlearning harmful behaviors and learning new behaviors and perspectives. The process of creating a more objective lens to view my behavior and my relationship with Martel and Greyson has been critical.

When I am in the mode of "Martel (or Greyson) always does X," hearing a more objective view from another person or through writing can allow me to let go of my reactions while acknowledging my feelings.

The shift to respectful parenting can, ironically, be challenging for children as well. Just as students who are used to a teacher-dominated classroom can resist a model of teaching that embraces their own experiences and thoughts, children may not know how to react to the changes in how we treat them. If we've been controlling and dominating for a long period of time, it will take time for them to regain trust in our desire to connect to them. They may wonder if we have ulterior motives and are manipulating them. Important in my own process is the ability to own my mistakes from the past and acknowledge them to Martel and Greyson while I'm working toward a different way of relating to them.

Passion

Tapping into our motivation and passion to create supportive, respectful, empowering relationships with children can help us during tough moments. Being on this path—learning, unlearning, engaging in reflection, and challenging ourselves through the transformative learning process—can be difficult. If we remember why we're on this path and can remain connected to our passion about this kind of work, we can sustain ourselves through moments of doubt.

Finding joy, hope, and love in our parenting process can carry us through the times when we want to just give up. The task may seem impossible. Our surrounding environments may push us to fall back into old patterns of behavior. Our childhood experiences may be triggering us and we may be reluctant to face up to them. Finding ways to tap into our passion keeps us moving forward while acknowledging and accepting our mistakes.

I look for solidarity among other parents struggling with creating freedom in their own lives. I talk with them about my struggles and I listen to theirs. We share in the journey. Sometimes I even find joy in the fact that I can face my mistakes and be accountable for the times I've exploded, lost it, and learned from it. Sometimes I can laugh at the ridiculousness of whatever the struggle is, like the one with Greyson over eight tiny, plastic penguins. Finding the humor and laughter—not at the expense of Martel and Greyson, but at my own missteps, mistakes, and ridiculousness— can move me back into finding my passion to go forward.

Another way to maintain this passion is for me to take breaks away from this work. I don't always want to be thinking, writing, and analyzing. Often, I can just be. I can go see a movie by myself. I can exercise. I can read something hilarious and laugh out loud. I can watch a dumb movie and laugh at fart jokes.

The other way to continue to cultivate passion for change is to just feel what we feel, to let go of fighting the fact that I "shouldn't" feel angry about the penguins or going to Wal-Mart. I need to feel how I feel and be with those feelings, just as I might be with Martel and Greyson, without judgment and without the need to change anything at that moment.

I can be angry and frustrated with Martel or Greyson, and still treat them with respect. I can redefine the way anger looked in my childhood. I can realize that the feelings themselves are not the things I need to change. Acknowledging and accepting all the parts of myself in the same way that I want to accept all the parts of Greyson and Martel is part of my goal as a parent. So I can feel the judgments, feel the feelings, and just let them be a part of who I am at that moment.

Finding the moments of joy in everyday, mundane tasks also reignites my passion. I stop, I breathe, I look, and I listen without judgment, with an open heart and mind. Being mindful and appreciating even those tasks I was socialized to view as a "chore" reminds me that joy is all around me.

Finally, I am inspired by the passion in Martel and Greyson. I take a moment to look in their eyes. I stop and really see them. Perhaps it's the moment when Martel is eating something he really loves. Maybe it's watching Greyson snap his fingers and dance in his chair while watching a music video. I stop the tasks I'm busy doing and see him—not the hair that needs to be brushed or the shirt that needs to be washed, just him in all his joy and presence.

Looking to the children who share our lives and watching the ways in which their own passions are sparked when they experience freedom to explore who they are in the world can help us remember why we do what we do.

CHAPTER SIX

Conclusion

AT THE BEGINNING of this journey I asked you to take what may have seemed like a leap of faith. I asked you to stay with me and see the possibilities of changing our views of children and childhood. A leap of faith, however, refers to a belief in something that cannot be proven. At the end of this book, I ask us to remember that we've seen the evidence that shows how harmful control is to children and their development. That evidence resides not only in research, but also in our own experiences as children and adults.

In spite of all of the evidence to the contrary, our culture has asked us to take on faith that control is an indispensable parenting tool. I ask us now to reject the leap of faith our culture encouraged us to take.

By examining the ways in which our culture and society construct and define childhood, we can engage in the process of examining our unquestioned assumptions about children and control. We may have experienced harmful control ourselves as children. We can embrace those experiences for what they truly were and commit to being with children in a different way. We can choose to understand how those experiences shaped our own views and behaviors as parents. We can choose to move forward. As parents, we can choose to be on the frontlines of change. We can choose to change our frame of reference and reject cultural norms of control and domination of children.

Changing our frame of reference about children not only has a profound impact on our relationships with children, it can begin to shift our broader cultural norms and ideas away from control and domination. How does it do this? By redefining childhood and the adult/child relationship, we give today's children a different frame of reference. The assumptions they take on about the world end up being radically different from the assumptions we learned. It is an intriguing idea: can we really create powerful social change just by changing how we view childhood?

In the last two centuries in the U.S., we've witnessed the kind of social change that comes from changing how we view groups of people and acting from that new point of view. By changing our dominant assumptions about the capabilities and rights of people from various social groups based on gender, race, sexual orientation, ability status, and ethnicity, we've seen how we can effect changes in cultural institutions and access to cultural resources. Our society today has by no means achieved equality or eliminated discrimination, but it has moved forward in realizing some measure of positive change for the less powerful in our society.

If we begin to change our view of children and childhood, perhaps we can finally get to the source of discrimination and oppression. Children learn potent lessons about power. Even when we think the lesson is about sharing or not hitting a sibling, what they learn is about power.

When they are treated with disregard and disrespect because they are little, they learn powerlessness. They learn what it feels like to be treated as less than human, and they learn that children in our society are meant to be treated in that way. When they are treated with respect, they learn what it means to be regarded as human and deserving of respect. Instead of a world in which the more powerful have control over the less powerful, we can create an expectation about life that affirms the dignity of all human beings, a world where children grow up with the internalized belief and experience that each individual deserves to be treated with respect.

Take a moment to imagine a culture, a society, and a world where children never have the experience of being controlled by those who are more powerful. Imagine a world where children believe that each person has the right to be trusted and respected. Imagine a world where mistrust, power-over dynamics, domination, and oppression no longer exist because children have never experienced them. Because they don't have these harmful experiences, they no longer have the ability or the desire to create— or rather perpetuate—these experiences on those who are less powerful.

By the simple, but often challenging, act of redefining our relationships with children, we can begin the process of creating profound social change. We can create a different world by taking the steps we need to shift our thinking, our behavior, and our views of how the world works for children.

This journey isn't just about the research or the empirical evidence that supporting and respecting children is better than controlling them. This journey is also about our hearts. At its core, parenting is about love. It can be about love that is based in fear and control or love that is based in trust and respect. When we're connected to children, when we're present and mindful with children, when we're operating from a place of love and trust with children, we feel good. We feel that things are right. Our hearts tell us when we're connected from a place of love, not fear.[1]

The children who share our lives give us the opportunity to transform ourselves so that they can transform the world. They call to us to change, and we need to recognize that call. It may be in what we would have formerly called rebellion. It may be in their tears. It may be in their silent suffering. It may be in the love, joy, and laughter they share with us when they are free from domination and control. We can share in that joy as children free us from the control and domination we have accepted as a natural part of life.

No matter what our relationships in the past have been, with our own parents and the children in our lives, we're capable of making this amazing shift and transformation. We engage in this process for ourselves and for the children in our lives, with the belief that we can create change in the world.

It would be a lie to say that I don't have hopes and dreams for Greyson and Martel. I do. I see freedom and liberation in their lives. I hope that they experience a world that allows them to express all the aspects of who they are with acceptance and love. I hope that they live their lives knowing that they can choose to explore thoughts, emotions, dreams, passions, and commitments without limits.

I hope that they continue to feel the ups and downs of life while being true to who they are. I hope that they feel free to follow their passions, if they so desire. I hope that they will find and embrace their commonalities and differences with others. I hope that they create for others the same freedom they have within themselves. My biggest hope for them is that they are who they want to be.

As we move forward on this journey of radical change and transformation together, we can look to the children who share our lives and know that they are the change the world needs. My hope is that all children are able to be who they want to be in the world, to live life authentically, and to find their passions. Just as we are each reflections of the world, the world is changed by our commitment to liberation and freedom.

FURTHER READING

Many wonderful books, articles, and websites have been written about gentle parenting and the kinds of personal growth advocated in this book. The works below have been selected because they offer evidence-based discussions of issues that are often "hot button" topics for parents trying to release controls.

Gerard Jones, *Killing Monsters: Why Children Need Fantasy, Super Heroes, and Make-Believe Violence* (2003), helps parents learn to differentiate between what violent games mean to children and what they mean to adults, and stop imposing their understanding of them on children. Adults may be horrified at the literal meaning of a video game, but children are far more interested in its emotional meaning.

Alfie Kohn, *Unconditional Parenting* (2005) and *Punished by Rewards* (1999), challenges us to think about what children need and how we meet those needs, rather than how we can get children to do what we tell them. He also makes the case against using rewards with students, children, and employees, offering alternatives to traditional carrot-and-stick practices at school, at home, and at work.

Gordon Neufeld, *Hold on to your kids: Why parents need to matter more than peers* (2006), offers effective strategies for preserving and restoring the child-to-parent relationship. It offers refreshing natural alternatives to today's contrived methods of behavior control.

Meredith Small, *Our Babies, Ourselves: How Biology and Culture Shape the Way We Parent* (1999) and *Kids: How Biology and Culture Shape the Way We Raise Our Children* (2002), looks at the intersection of biology and culture in the evolution of human behavior, in particular how biology and culture influence parenting styles. She challenges some of the "truths" we have come to accept about parenting.

NOTES

Introduction

[1] William Sears, *What Attachment Parenting Is: The 7 Baby B's*, AskDrSears.com, http://www.askdrsears.com/html/10/t130300.asp, (December 1, 2010).

Chapter 1 – Dynamics of Control

[1] Dictionary.com, http://dictionary.reference.com/browse/power (December 22, 2010).

[2] Dictionary.com, http://dictionary.reference.com/browse/control (December 22, 2010).

[3] Bobbi Harro, "The Cycle of Socialization" in Maurianne Adams, ed, *Readings in Diversity and Social Justice* (New York, NY, Routledge 2000), 16. See also Stephen A. Grunland and Marvin K. Mayers, *Enculturation and Acculturation: A Reading for Cultural Anthropology*, http://home.snu.edu/~hculbert/encultur.htm, (December 26, 2010).

[4] Harro, 16.

[5] Doris Buhler-Niederberger, "Introduction: Childhood Sociology, Defining the State of the Art and Ensuring Reflection," *Current Sociology*, 2010 58: 159-160.

[6] Grunland and Mayers.

[7] Grunland and Mayers, and Harro, 16.

[8] Buhler-Niederberger, 156.

[9] Clea A. McNeely and Brian K. Barber, "How Do Parents Make Adolescents Feel Loved? Perspectives on Supportive Parenting from Adolescents in 12 Cultures," *Journal of Adolescent Research* (January 2010): 607.

[10] For an in-depth cross-cultural look at child-rearing and the impact of culture on parenting norms, see Meredith Small's *Kids: How Biology and Culture Shape the Way We Raise Our Children*, Doubleday 2001. Small challenges us to look more deeply at our cultural assumptions about how to raise children and the impact of those assumptions on children.

[11] Barry Checkoway, *Adults as Allies*, W.K. Kellogg Foundation, http://www.wkkf.org/knowledge-center/resources/2001/12/Adults-As-Allies.aspx (July 5, 2010) 13.

[12] Ronald Takaki, *A Different Mirror: A History of Multicultural America* (New York, NY: Back Bay Books/Little, Brown and Company, 2008) 45, 82, 101, and 131.

[13] Andrew Jackson, in various correspondences during the year 1829, referred to himself as a "father" and native people as his Indian "children." If those "…children refused to accept his advice, they would be responsible for the consequences." Takaki, 82.

[14] Arlen C. Moller and Edward L. Deci, "Interpersonal control, dehumanization, and violence: A self-determination theory perspective," *Group Processes and Intergroup Relations* 41 (January 2010): 41.

[15] Michal Kanat-Maymon and Avi Assor, "Perceived Maternal Control and Responsiveness to Distress as Predictors of Young Adults' Empathic Responses," *Personality and Social Psychology Bulletin* (October 2009): 34.

Chapter 2 – Ways We Control Children

[1] Checkoway, 13.

[2] William Roberts and Janet Strayer, "Parents' Responses to the Emotional Distress of their Children: Relations with Children's Competence," *Developmental Psychology,* 1987, 23, 17, http://www.tru.ca/faculty/wlroberts/index.html#papers.

[3] William L. Roberts, "The socialization of emotional expression: relations with prosocial behaviour and competence in five samples," *Canadian Journal of Behavioural Science,* 1999, 31, 6, http://www.tru.ca/faculty/wlroberts/index.html#papers.

[4] Charles Darwin, as quoted in Doris Cope, "Neonatal Pain: The Evolution of an Idea" in *American Society of Anesthesiologists Newsletter,* September 1998, Vol 62, http://asatest.asahq.org/Newsletters/1998/09_98/Neonatal_0998.html, (January 1, 2011).

[5] Howard J. Stang and Leonard W. Snellman "Circumcision Practice Patterns in the United States" in *Pediatrics, The Official Journal of the American Academy of Pediatrics,* 1998,101, e5, 1.

[6] Stang and Snellman, 2.

[7] Cope.

[8] John Holt, *How Children Learn,* (New York, NY, Perseus 1983), 44.

[9] Jonathan P. Schwartz, Sally M. Hage, Imelda Bush, and Lauren Key Burns, "Unhealthy Parenting and Potential Mediators As Contributing Factors To Future Intimate Violence : A Review of the Literature," *Trauma, Violence, and Abuse* 2006 7, 208.

[10] Ibid.

[11] Ibid.

[12] William Sears, *Shaping Young Tastes*, AskDr.Sears.com, http://www.askdrsears.com/html/3/T031900.asp (August 1, 2010).

[13] Silvia Scaglioni, Michela Salvioni, and Cinzia Galimberti, "Influence of parental attitudes in the development of children eating behaviour," *British Journal of Nutrition* 2008, 99. Suppl. 1, S23.

[14] Trish Murray, "Wait Not, Want Not: Factors Contributing to the Development of Anorexia Nervosa and Bulimia Nervosa," *The Family Journal* (July 2003), 278.

[15] Sylvia Kerr, *Fundamentals of Feeding Children*, National Eating Disorder Information Centre, 3, http://www.nedic.ca/resources/IndexofArticlesbySubject.shtml (July 3, 2010).

[16] Harro, 20.

[17] Christopher J. Ferguson, Stephanie Rueda, Amanda D. Cruz, Diana E. Ferguson, and Stacey Fritz, "Violent Video Games and Aggression: Causal Relationship or Byproduct of Family Violence and Intrinsic Violence Motivation?" *Criminal Justice and Behavior*, 2008 35: 330.

[18] For further exploration of the important role that violent games can play in children's lives, see Gerard Jones' excellent book, *Killing Monsters: Why Children Need Fantasy, Super Heroes and Make-Believe Violence* (2002).

[19] Cheryl K. Olson, Lawrence A. Kutner, and Dorothy E. Warner, "The Role of Violent Video Game Content in Adolescent Development: Boys' Perspectives," *Journal of Adolescent Research* 2008 23, 69.

[20] Stephanie S. VanDeventer and James A. White, "Expert Behavior in Children's Video Game Play," *Simulation Gaming* 2002 33, 29.

[21] VanDeventer and White, 46.

[22] Rita Hardiman and Bailey Jackson, "Conceptual Foundations for Social Justice Education" in Maurianne Adams, Lee Anne Bell, and Pat Griffin, eds,

Teaching for Diversity and Social Justice, (New York, NY, Routledge 2007), 37.

[23] See for example, Scaglioni, Salvioni, and Galimberti, S24, and Moller and Deci, 42.

[24] Kanat-Maymon and Assor, 42.

[25] For more information about the harm of conditional parenting, see Alfie Kohn's *Punished by Rewards (1999)*.

[26] Paulo Freire, *Pedagogy of the Oppressed: 30th Anniversary Edition*, (New York, NY, Continuum International Publishing Group, Limited, 2006) 147.

[27] As a family, we have embraced a philosophy of learning that is often referred to as unschooling. John Holt first used this term in the 1970's. For more information on unschooling see John Holt's Growing Without Schooling website, http://www.holtgws.com/whatisunschoolin.html, and this general site on unschooling, http://www.unschooling.com/library/faq/index.shtml, as well as Sandra Dodd's site, http://www.sandradodd.com/unschooling (which includes information on radical unschooling).

[28] John Holt spent most of the 1950's and 1960's as a teacher in private schools. In the 1960's he wrote his two most popular books, *How Children Fail* (1964) and *How Children Learn* (1967), based on his experiences as a teacher and keen observer of children. He eventually embraced homeschooling as a legitimate option for children and continued to advocate for trusting children to live and learn both in and out of school in their own unique ways. See http://www.holtgws.com/johnholtpage.html.

[29] John Holt, *How Children Fail*, (New York, NY: Pittman Publishing, 1964) 156.

[30] Holt, *How Children Fail*, 17-18.

[31] For more information about how rewards and conditional approval by teachers and parents create fear and are ineffective motivators, see Alfie Kohn's *Punished by Rewards* (1999) and *Unconditional Parenting* (2005).

[32] Holt, *How Children Fail*, 49.

[33] As a schoolteacher for nearly 30 years in New York City, John Taylor Gatto was named New York City Schoolteacher of the Year three times and New York State Schoolteacher of the Year once before he quit teaching in 1991. He has gone on to a public speaking career and authored numerous books on school reform, including *The Underground History of American Education* (2006) and *Dumbing Us Down: The Hidden Curriculum of Compulsory Schooling* (1991). See http://www.johntaylorgatto.com/aboutus/john.htm.

[34] John Taylor Gatto, *The Underground History of American Education*, Rev. ed, (Oxford, NY: The Oxford Village Press, 2006) 386.

[35] Gatto, 309.

[36] Holt, *How Children Fail*, 136.

[37] Gatto, 44-45.

[38] Gatto, 45.

Chapter 3 – Controlling Parenting versus Supportive Parenting

[1] Moller and Deci, 50.

[2] Catrin Finkenauer, Rutger C.M.E. Engels, and Roy F. Baumeister, "Parenting behaviour and adolescent behavioural and emotional problems: The role of self control," *International Journal of Behavioral Development*, 2005 29, 66.

[3] McNeely and Barber, 604.

[4] Scaglioni, Salvioni, and Galimberti, S24.

[5] Moller and Deci, 42.

[6] Kanat-Maymon and Assor, 34.

[7] Kanat-Maymon and Assor, 42.

[8] Thomas G. Patterson and Stephen Joseph, "Person-Centered Personality Theory: Support from Self-Determination Theory and Positive Psychology," *Journal of Humanistic Psychology* 2007 47, 125 and 130-131.

[9] Moller and Deci, 42.

[10] Holt, *How Children Fail*, 140.

[11] For a more thorough exploration of the impact of conditional parenting, see Alfie Kohn's *Unconditional Parenting* (2005); see Gordon Neufeld's *Hold on to your kids: Why parents need to matter more than peers* (2006) for more information on the importance of a connected parental relationship to children during adolescence.

[12] Stephen Brookfield, "Repositioning Ideology Critique in a Critical Theory of Adult Learning," *Adult Education Quarterly* 2001 52, 17.

[13] Finkenauer, Engels, and Baumeister, 66.

[14] McNeely and Barber, 604.

[15] McNeely and Barber, 606 and Patterson and Joseph, 125 and 130-131.

[16] Ibid.

[17] Moller and Deci, 42.

[18] Andrew J. Supple, Sharon R. Ghazarian, Gary W. Peterson and Kevin R. Bush, "Assessing the Cross-Cultural Validity of a Parental Autonomy Granting Measure: Comparing Adolescents in the United States, China, Mexico, and India," *Journal of Cross-Cultural Psychology* 2009 40, 818.

[19] Kanat-Maymon and Assor, 34.

[20] Supple, Ghazarian, Peterson, and Bush, 818, 830-831.

[21] Eva M. Pomerantz and Qian Wang, "The Role of Parental Control in Children's Development in Western and East Asian Countries," *Current Directions in Psychological Science* 2009 18, 288.

[22] Buhler-Niederberger, 156.

[23] Ibid.

[24] Angie Williams, "Adolescents' Relationships With Parents," *Journal of Language and Social Psychology* 2003 22, 63.

Chapter 4 – Steps Toward Liberation and Freedom

[1] Freire, *Pedagogy of the Oppressed*, 56.

[2] Bobbi Harro, "The Cycle of Liberation," in Maurianne Adams, ed, *Readings in Diversity and Social Justice* (New York, NY, Routledge 2000), 464.

[3] Mark K. Smith, *David A. Kolb on Experiential Learning,* infed.org, http://www.infed.org/biblio/b-explrn.htm (August 8, 2010).

[4] Harro, "The Cycle of Liberation," 463.

[5] Barbara Love, "Developing a Liberatory Consciousness," in Maurianne Adams, ed, *Readings in Diversity and Social Justice* (New York, NY, Routledge 2000), 470.

[6] Love, 474.

[7] Love, 471.

[8] Freire, 79.

Chapter 5 – Tools for Transformation and Change

[1] Patricia Cranton and Merv Roy, "When the Bottom Falls Out of the Bucket: Toward A Holistic Perspective on Transformative Learning," *Journal of Transformative Education* 2003 1, 87-88.

[2] Cranton and Roy, 91.

[3] Cranton and Roy, 95.

[4] Cranton and Roy, 96-97.

[5] Cranton and Roy, 94.

[6] Nirbhay N. Singh, Giulio E. Lancioni, Alan S.W. Winton, John Curtis, Robert G. Wahler, and Kristen McAleavey, "Mindful Parenting Decreases Aggression and Increases Social Behavior in Children with Developmental Disabilities," *Journal of Emotional and Behavioral Disorders* 2006 14, 764.

[7] Ibid.

[8] Ibid.

[9] See the section on Further Reading for a list of resources.

[10] Margaret Shih, Elsie Wang, Amy Trahan Bucher and Rebecca Stotzer, "Perspective Taking: Reducing Prejudice Towards General Outgroups and Specific Individuals," *Group Processes and Intergroup Relations*, 2009 12, 565.

[11] Love, 470.

[12] Raymond Scurfield, *Survival Strategies in War and Bringing Them Home*, Patriot Outreach, http://www.patriotoutreach.org/survival-strategies.html (September 22, 2010).

[13] For more information on EFT, see http://www.eftuniverse.com/.

[14] For more information on Byron Katie's The Work, see http://www.thework.com/index.php.

Chapter 6 - Conclusion

[1] To further explore joyful parenting, see Scott Noelle's work at www.enjoyparenting.com.